Pocke
Mu

All of the important music terms clearly defined, including the language of music notation, music theory, signs and abbreviations, famous composers' dates, and more.

Amsco Publications
New York/London/Paris/Sydney/Copenhagen/Madrid

Cover photograph by SuperStock
Project editor: Peter Pickow
Interior design and layout: Len Vogler

This book Copyright © 1999 by Amsco Publications,
A Division of Music Sales Corporation, New York

All rights reserved. No part of this book may be
reproduced in any form or by any electronic or mechanical means,
including information storage and retrieval systems,
without permission in writing from the publisher.

Order No. AM 948970
US International Standard Book Number: 0.8256.1716.2
UK International Standard Book Number: 0.7119.7604.X

Exclusive Distributors:
Music Sales Corporation
257 Park Avenue South, New York, NY 10010 USA
Music Sales Limited
8/9 Frith Street, London W1V 5TZ England
Music Sales Pty. Limited
120 Rothschild Street, Rosebery, Sydney, NSW 2018, Australia

Printed in the United States of America by
Vicks Lithograph and Printing Corporation

Music Notation

Music notation is written on a *staff* of five lines and four spaces. Leger lines are added above and below the staff for notes extending beyond the staff.

Notes are placed on the staff to indicate the tones to be sounded. Different kinds of notes indicate duration or time value. Each note has a corresponding *rest* that means the same duration of silence.

	Note	Rest	
Whole	𝅝	𝄻	
Half	𝅗𝅥	𝄼	
Quarter	𝅘𝅥	𝄽	
Eighth	𝅘𝅥𝅮	𝄾	𝅘𝅥𝅮𝅘𝅥𝅮
Sixteenth	𝅘𝅥𝅯	𝄿	𝅘𝅥𝅯𝅘𝅥𝅯
Thirty-second	𝅘𝅥𝅰	𝅀	𝅘𝅥𝅰𝅘𝅥𝅰
Sixty-fourth	𝅘𝅥𝅱	𝅁	

Clef signs are placed at the beginning of each staff to indicate pitch. The most commonly used are the *Treble* (G clef) and the *Bass* (F clef).

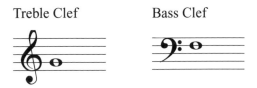

The C clef may be written on any of three different lines to indicate the position of Middle C.

A treble staff and a bass staff joined together form a *grand staff*.

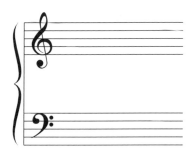

A *time signature* is placed on the staff at the beginning of each piece or section. The top number means how many beats in each measure; the bottom number means what kind of a note receives one beat. Bar lines divide the staff into measures.

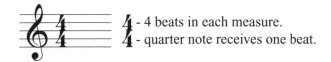

4 - 4 beats in each measure.
4 - quarter note receives one beat.

Some commonly-used Time Signatures:

$\frac{2}{4} \quad \frac{3}{4} \quad \frac{4}{4} \quad \frac{5}{4} \quad \frac{6}{4} \quad \frac{9}{8} \quad \frac{3}{8} \quad \frac{6}{8} \quad \frac{7}{8} \quad \frac{12}{8} \quad \frac{3}{2} \quad \frac{2}{2}$

Special Time Signatures:

$C = \frac{4}{4} \qquad ₵ = \frac{2}{2}$

Chromatic Signs

Sharp, flat, and natural signs are placed before notes to alter their pitch.
The sharp ♯ raises the note one-half step.
The flat ♭ lowers the note one-half step.
The natural ♮ cancels a sharp or flat and restores the note to its original pitch.
The double sharp ✕ raises the note one whole step.
The double flat ♭♭ lowers the note one whole step.

When the chromatic signs are used within the piece of music, they are called *accidentals*. When all notes of a certain letter name are to be sharp or flat, they are placed at the beginning of each staff and are called the *key signature*.

Key Signatures

C major or A minor

G major or E minor

D major or B minor

A major or F♯ minor

E major or C♯ minor

B major or G♯ minor

F♯ major or D♯ minor

C♯ major or A♯ minor

F major or D minor

B♭ major or G minor

E♭ major or C minor

A♭ major or F minor

D♭ major or B♭ minor

G♭ major or E♭ minor

C♭ major or A♭ minor

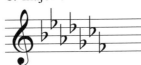

Key Circle

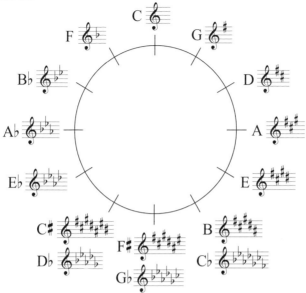

Intervals

An interval is the distance in pitch between two tones, counted by degree on the staff. Usually the degrees are counted from the lower note up to the higher note. Intervals have both a number name and a quality name. Intervals may be Perfect (P), Major (M), Minor (m), Augmented (aug), or Diminished (dim).

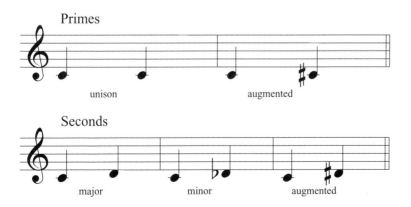

Chart of Common Chords

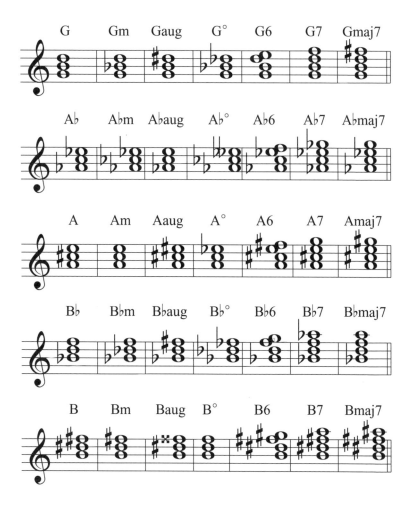

Scales

A *scale* (Latin, *scala,* meaning ladder) is a series of tones in a pattern of whole steps and half steps. Scales are the tonal material used by composers. The possibilities of various combinations within the chromatic octave are endless. The most commonly used scales are:

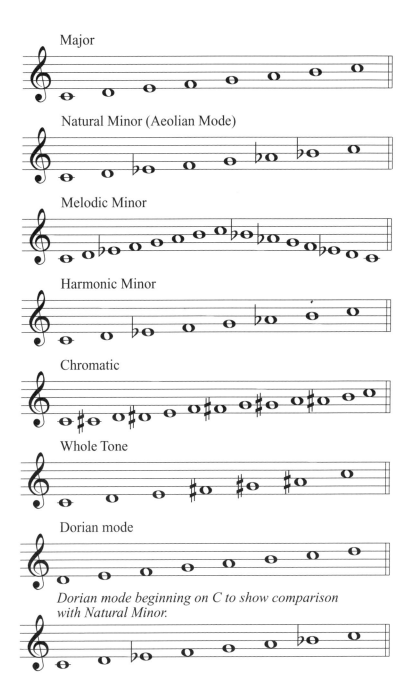

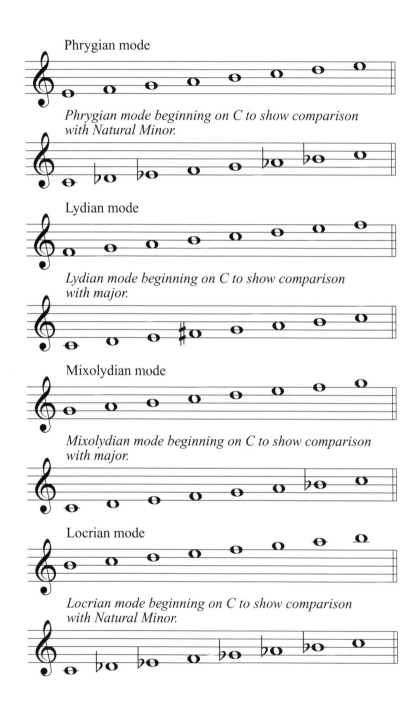

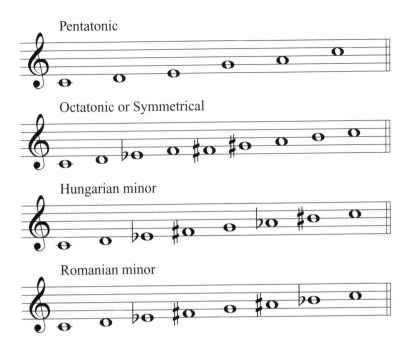

Scale Degree Names

Each tone or degree of a diatonic scale has a specific name. They may also indicated by Roman numerals that show the kind of triad that is built on each degree. The following chart is for a Major Key:

Tonic	I (Major)
Super Tonic	ii (minor)
Mediant	iii
Subdominant	IV
Dominant	V
Submediant	vi
(Subtonic)	VII (lowered 7th degree)
Leading Tone	vii (diminished)

Scale degree names of the Melodic Minor Scale (including all the degrees of the Natural and Harmonic Scales):

Ascending:

Tonic	i
Supertonic	ii
Mediant	III+ (Augmented)
Subdominant	IV
Dominant	V
Raised Submediant	vi°
Leading Tone	vii°
Tonic	viii

Descending:

Subtonic	VII
Submediant	VI
Dominant	v
Subdominant	iv
Mediant	III
Supertonic	ii°
Tonic	i

Signs

> ∧	accented, emphasized.
⸘	arpeggio.
.	1. A dot over or under a note indicates staccato.
	2. A dot following a note or rest increased the value of that note or rest by one-half.
V	Up-bow.
⊓	Down-bow.
⌒	Hold, fermata.
𝄋	Segno. Repeat from this sign.
♮	Natural.
♯	Sharp.
x	Double sharp.
♭	Flat.
♭♭	Double flat.
⌣	Slur, tie.
./.	Repeat.
⊕	Coda mark. Sign is disregarded the first time through, but the second time the performer skips from the sign to the coda.

∪	Heel, in organ playing.
∧	Toe, in organ playing.
<	Crescendo
>	Diminuendo
⌢	Bebung

Abbreviations

Accel.	Accelerando
Acc. or accomp.	Accompaniment
Adg° or Ad°.	Adagio
Ad lib.	Ad libitum
Affett.	Affettuoso
Affrett.	Affrettando
Ag° or Agit°.	Agitato
All°.	Allegro
All' ott.	All' ottava
All' 8va.	All' ottava
Al seg.	Al segno
And.	Andantino
And.	Andante
Anim°.	Animato
Arc.	Arcato
Arp°.	Arpeggio
A tem. or A temp.	A tempo
B.C.	Basso continuo
Br.	Bratsche
Brill.	Brillante
C.a.	Coll'arco
Cad.	Cadenza
Cal.	Calando
Cantab.	Cantabile
C.B.	Contra basso
C.D.	Colla destra
Cello.	Violoncello
C.f.	Cantus firmus
Ch.	Choir Organ
C.L.	Col legno
Cl., or Clar.	Clarinet
Clar°.	Clarino
Coll'ott or C. 8va.	Coll' ottava

15

Cor.	Cornet
C.P.	Colla parte
Cresc.	Crescendo
C.S.	Colla sinistra
C. voc.	Colla Voce
Dal. S.	Dal segno
D.C.	Da capo
Decresc.	Decrescendo
Diap.	Diapason
Dim.	Diminuendo
Div.	Divisi
Dol.	Dolce
D.S.	Dal segno
Esp.	Espressivo
Fag.	Fagotto
ff.	Fortissimo
fff.	Fortississimo
Fl.	Flute
Flag.	Flageolet
F.O.	Full Organ
fp.	Forte piano
Fortz. or fz.	Forzato or forzando
G.O.	Great Organ
G.P.	General pause
Graz.	Grazioso
Gsp.	Glockenspiel
Gt.	Great Organ
Haut.	Hautboy
Hptw.	Hauptwerk
Hr.	Horn
Intro.	Introduction
Inv.	Inversion
Leg.	Legato
Legg.	Leggiero
L.H.	Left hand
Marc.	Marcato
M.d.	Mano destra
Men.	Meno
Mez.	Mezzo
mf.	Mezzo forte

M.g.	Main gauche
M.M.	Maelzel's Metronome
Mod.	Moderato
Mor.	Morendo
mp.	Mezzo piano
MS.	Manuscript
M.s.	Mano sinistra
M.v.	Mezza voce
Ob.	Oboe
Ob.	Obbligato
Op.	Opus
Org.	Organ
Ott. or 8va.	Ottava
p.	Piano
Ped.	Pedal
Perd.	Perdendosi
Pes.	Pesante
Pf.	Piu forte
P.F.	Pianoforte
Pizz.	Pizzicato
pp, ppp.	Pianissimo
Rall.	Rallentando
Recit.	Recitative
Rf.	Rinforzando
R.H.	Right hand
Rit.	Ritardando
Ritard.	Ritardando
Riten.	Ritenuto
Scherz.	Scherzando
Seg.	Segue
Sem. or Semp.	Sempre
sf.	Sforzando
Sim.	Simile
Sin.	Sinistra
Sinf.	Sinfonia
Smorz.	Smorzando
Sost.	Sostenuto
Stacc.	Staccato
Stent.	Stendando
St. Diap.	Stopped Diapason

S.T.	Senza tempo
Sw.	Swell Organ
Sym.	Symphony
T.C.	Tre corde
Temp.	Tempo
Ten.	Tenuto
Timp.	Timpani
Tpt.	Trumpet
Tr.	Trill
Trem.	Tremulant
Tromb.	Trombone
T.S.	Tasto solo
U.C.	Una corda
Unis.	Unisoni
Va.	Viola
Var.	Variation
Vc., Vcl., Vcllo.	Violoncello
V.S.	Volti subito
Viv.	Vivace
Vv.	Violins

Tempo Terms

Steady Rate Of Speed

Grave	solemnly, slowly
Largo	very slow, stately
Larghetto	quite slow, broad
Lento	slowly
Adagio	slowly, with expression
Adagietto	slightly faster than Adagio
Andantino	usually slower than Andante, sometimes faster
Andante	moving, walking speed
Moderato	moderately, medium speed
Allegretto	moving, but slower than Allegro
Allegro	lively, animated
Vivace	animated, faster than allegro
Vivo	lively, brisk
Presto	fast
Prestissimo	very fast

Speeding Up

Accelerando	gradually faster
Affrettando	hurrying, sometimes temporarily
Doppio movimento	twice as fast
Incalzando	with more warmth and fervor
Piu mosso	more movement
Piu moto	more movement
Stringendo	hurrying, speeding up
Veloce	greatly increased speed
Velocissimo	with great velocity

Slowing Down

Allargando	ritarding and broadening
Calando	gradually slower and softer
Meno mosso	less speed
Meno moto	less speed
Molto meno mosso	with much less speed
Morendo	dying away by degrees
Rallentando	slower, but not softer
Ritardando	gradually slower
Slargando	gradually slower
Slentando	slackening, slowing down
Sminuendo	slower and softer
Smorzando	slower and softer
Strascinando	gradually slower
Tardando	gradually slower

Terms for both *tempo* and *dynamics*

Allargando	growing broader and slower
Calando	gradually softer and slower
Morendo	fading away
Perdendo	getting lost, fading away
Sminuendo	slower and softer
Smorzando	fading away

Dynamic Terms

Crescendo	increasing, gradually louder
Decrescendo	gradually softer, decreasing
Diluendo	growing softer
Diminuendo	diminishing, gradually softer
Forte	loud
Fortepiano	attack loudly, sustain softly
Fortissimo	very load
Mezzo forte	moderately loud
Mezzo piano	moderately soft
Piano	soft
Pianissimo	very soft

Expression Terms

Affanato	sad, distressed
Affettuoso	tender
Amabile	amiable, gentle
Amorevole	loving, gentle
Animato	animated, spirited
Appassionato	passionate, much feeling
Ardito	boldly
Ardore	with warmth, ardor
Bravura	skill, dexterity
Brillante	sparkling, showy
Brio	vigor, spirit
Calma	quiet, tranquil
Calore	warmth
Cantabile	in a singing style
Capriccioso	capricious, fanciful
Deciso	bold, determined
Dolce	sweet, mild
Dolendo	sorrowful
Espressivo	expressive
Forzando	force, strength
Fuoco	fire
Furioso	furious, wild
Giocoso	playful, humorous
Gioioso	joy, cheer
Intrepido	bold
Maestoso	majestic, stately

Marcia	march
Mesto	sad
Misterioso	mysteriously
Nobilemente	grand, lofty, noble
Placido	calm, tranquil
Pomposo	pompous
Preciso	precise, exact
Religioso	religious, devotional
Risoluto	resolute, firm
Robusto	firm, bold
Scherzando	(in a) playful manner
Scherzo	joke
Scioto	easy, free
Semplice	simple, unaffected
Sentimento	sentiment, feeling
Sentito	expressive
Sereno	serene
Spiritoso	spirited
Strepitoso	noisy, boisterous
Teneramente	tenderly, delicately
Tranquillo	tranquil, quiet
Vago	vague, dreamy

Tonal Production Terms

A due corde	on two strings, soft pedal depressed halfway (piano)
A tre corde	on three strings, without soft pedal (piano)
A una corde	on one string, soft pedal completely depressed (piano)
Forzando	forced, strongly accented
Legato	bound, smoothly connected
Leggero	light, swift, delicate
Leggiero	light, swift, delicate
Marcando	marked, with emphasis
Marcato	marked, with emphasis
Pesante	heavy, ponderous
Pieno	full
Portamento	sliding from one tone to another
Portato	half staccato
Sforzando	strongly accented, forced

Sforzato	accented, forced
Sostenuto	sustained
Spiccato	separated, detached
Staccato	detached
Tenuto	sustained, held full value

Other Terms

Al fine	to the end
Al segno	to the sign
A piacere	at one's pleasure, freely
Con	with
Da capo	repeat from the beginning
Da capo al fine	repeat from the beginning to the end; to Fine
Dal Segno al fine	repeat from the sign to the end
Fine	end
Mano destra	right hand
Mano sinistra	left hand
Meno	less
Molto	much
Non	not
Più	more
Poco a poco	little by little, gradually
Primo	first
Segue	continue without pause
Sempre	always
Senza	without
Simile	like
Stesso	same
Subito	immediately
Tasto solo	bass notes only, no accompaniment
Troppo	too much
Volti subito	turn the page over quickly

Pronunciation

This music dictionary uses a pronunciation system that eliminates the need for special symbols. Pronunciations are given as needed for Italian, French, and German words in the closest approximation in the English language. An acute mark (´) follows the stressed syllable.

In order to fit the word to English as nearly as possible, no special code is used. However, the following spellings are generally used for vowels:

       Example
       ay - late
       ah - far
       aw - all
       eh - get
       ee - see
       y - usually for i as in like
       i - in
       ou, ow - out
       oh - old
       oo - moo

A

A. (1) The first letter of the music alphabet. (2) The note from which the orchestra is tuned.
Ab (G). Off. used in organ music.
Abandon (F, ah-bahn-dohn′). Freely, without restraint.
A battuta (It, ah bah-too′tah). With the beat, strictly in time.
Abbellimenti (It). Embellishments, ornaments.
Abbreviations. See page 15.
Abendmusik (G. ah′bend-moo-zeek′). Evening musical performances.
Abnehmend (G, ahp′nay-mehn). Diminishing.
Absolute music. Music free from extra-musical implications; opposite of program music.
Abstract music. Same as Absolute Music.
Abstrich (G, ahp-streekh). Downbow.
Acalanto (Port). Brazilian cradle song.
A cappella (It, ah′kahp-pehl′lah). Without accompaniment.
A capriccio (It, ah-kah-pree-choh). In a fanciful, capricious style.
Accelerando (It, aht-chay-lay-rahn′doh). Becoming faster.
Accent. Stress or emphasis on a certain note or chord.
Acciaccatura (It, aht-chah-kah-too′rah). 'Crushing'. A very short grace note played with the principal note and immediately released.
Accidentals. Sharps, flats, and naturals used apart from the Key Signature.
Accolade (F). Brace.
Accompaniment. A secondary part or parts added to a principal part or voice.
Accopiato (It, ah-koh-pee-ah-toh). Bound, tied.
Accord (F). (1) Chord. (2) Way of tuning, especially of instruments such as the lute.
Accordatura (It, ahk-kor-dah-too′rah). Concord. The series of tones to which the open strings of an instrument are tuned.

Accordion-Aequalstimmen

Accordion. A portable musical instrument made of two headboards connected by folding bellows. Sound is produced by reeds vibrating freely inside the headboards. The right hand plays a piano keyboard while the left hand plays buttons that produce bass notes and chords. The earliest accordions were made by Buschmann in Germany (1822) and Damian in Italy (1829). Also see Concertina.
Accordo (It). Chord.
Accusé (F, ah-koo-zay′). With emphasis.
Achromatic. Diatonic.
Achtel (G, ahkh′tel). Eighth note.
Acoustics. (1) The qualities of a room or theatre which influence the transmission or the hearing of sounds. (2) The science of sound, as a branch of Physics.
Action. (1) Any kind of mechanism of an instrument that transmits the motion of the fingers or feet to the sound-producing parts. (2) The mechanism attached to the pedals of a harp that changes the pitch of the strings by shortening them.
Act Tune. Music played between the acts of a drama.
Adagietto (It, ah-dah-jee-eh′toh). (1) A tempo somewhat faster than adagio. (2) A short adagio.
Adagio (It, ah-dah′jee-oh). At ease, slow. A slow movement.
Adagissimo (It, ah-dah-jee′see-moh). Very slow.
Adaptation. Arrangement.
Added sixth. The sixth added to a triad.
Addolorato (It, ah-doh-loh-rah′toh). Sorrowful.
A demi jeu (F, ah dmee zhoo′). With half the power of the instrument.
A demi voix (F, ah dmee vwah′). At half voice.
A deux (F, ah doo). Duet.
Ad libitum. Abbr. ad lib. Freely, performer may improvise or vary the tempo. A part that may be omitted.
A due (It, ah doo′eh). In two parts. In wind parts, a single melodic line played by two instruments in unison. In string parts, a passage in two parts is played *divisi*.
Aeolian, Aeolian mode. See Modes.
Aeolian harp. An instrument of sound-box and strings so constructed that a current of air sets the strings in vibration.
Aequalstimmen (G). The eight foot pipes of the organ.

Aerophones-Allegretto

Aerophones. See Instruments.
Aesthetics of music. Philosophy or study of the beautiful.
Affabile (It, ahf-fah′bee′leh). Gentle, pleasing.
Affannato (It, ahf-fah-nah′toh). Sad, distressed.
Affannoso (It, ahf-fah-noh′soh). Anxious.
Affettuoso (It, ahf-feht-twaoh′soh). Tender. Passionate expression.
Afflitto (It, ahf-fleet′toh). Sorrowful, sad.
Affrettando (t, ahf-freht-tahn′doh). Hurrying.
Agevole (It, ah′jeh′voh′leh). Easy, smooth.
Agiatamente (It, ah-jah-tah-mehn′teh). Easily.
Agitato (It, ah-jee-tah′toh). Agitated, excited.
Agogic accent. One which is produced by duration, not by dynamic stress or pitch.
Agrements (F, ah-gray-mahn′). Ornaments.
Air. A tune or melody.
Aisis (G, ah′iss′iss). The note A double sharp.
Al (It), **a là** (F). At the; to the.
Alberti bass. A bass in broken chords.
Alborada (S, ahl-bhoh-rah′dah). A type of Spanish music, originally a morning song.
Albumblatt (G). Leaf or page or an album.
Album leaf. A short and simple piece.
Aleatory music. Music that has elements of chance in either the composition or the performance. Often called Chance Music. In composition, pitches, durations, degrees of intensity, etc., may be chosen by dice throwing, card drawing, abstract designs, mathematical laws of chance, or other means. In performance, chance is allowed by leaving some elements or their order of appearance to the performer's discretion. Form and structure are not definitely fixed so performances vary from one to another.
Al fine (It, ahl fee′neh). To the end.
Alla, all′ (It, ahl′lah). In the manner of.
Alla breve (It, ahl′lah breh′veh). A tempo mark meaning quick duple time with the half note receiving one beat.
Allargando (It, ahl-lahr-gahn′doh). Growing broader and slower.
Allegretto (It, ahl-leh-greht′toh). Light and cheerful; tempo between Andante and Allegro.

Allegro-Ancia

Allegro (It, ahl-lay'groh). Quick, lively.
Allemande (F, ahl-mahn'd). (1) A lively German dance in 2/4 time. (2) A German dance in 3/4 time. (3) A slow dance in 4/4 time. (4) A movement in the Suite, either first or following the Prelude.
Allentando (It, ahl-lehn-tahn'doh) Slower.
Allmählich (G, ahl-may'likh). Gradually.
Alt (It, ahlt). (1) Tones of the octave above the treble staff; said to be 'in air.' Tones of the next higher octave are said to be 'in altissimo.' (2) In German, the lower of the two female voices. With instruments, the second highest member of the family.
Alternativo (It, ahl-tair-nah-tee'voh). Alternating one movement with another.
Altistin (G, ahl'teest-in). A contralto singer.
Alto (It, ahl'toh). (1) Female voice of the lower range. (2) Second highest part of the usual four-part chorus. (3) Second highest instrument of the violin family. (4) Clarinet, flute, saxophone, etc., the third or fourth highest member of the family.
Alto clef. The C clef on the third line of the staff.
Altra volta (It). Encore.
Alzati (It, ahl-tsah'tee). Direction to remove the mutes.
Amabile (It, ah-mah'bee-leh). Gentle, with love.
Amen (Heb, 'so be it'). Often used at the end of hymns, prayers, and other sacred music.
Am Frosch (G). Direction to use the portion of the violin bow nearest the right hand.
Am Griffbrett (G). In violin playing, bowing near the fingerboard.
A moll (G). The Key of A minor.
Amore (It, ah-mor'ray). Love, affection.
Amorevole (It, ah-mor-ray'voh-leh). Lovingly.
Amplitude. The distance of a vibration, cycle.
Am Steg (G, ahm shtehk). In violin playing, bowing near the bridge.
Anacrusis (Greek, an-ah-kru'sis). Upbeat.
Analysis. Study of the form, structure, thematic material, melody, harmony, style, etc., of a composition.
Ancia (It). Reed.

Anche-Aperto

Anche (F, ahnsh). Reed organ stop.
Ancora (It, ahn-koh'rah). Once more, yet.
Andacht (G, ahn'dakht). Devotion.
Andante (It, ahn-dahn'teh). Moderate, graceful walking speed between Allegretto and Adagio.
Andantino (It, ahn-dahn-tee'noh). A short piece of andante tempo or character. When it is used to indicate tempo, it means a slight modification of Andante, either faster or slower.
Anfang, vom (G). From the beginning; same as Da Capo.
Anglaise (F, ahn-glez'). English country dance.
Angoscioso (It, ahn-goh-shoh'soh). Grieved, sorrowful.
Anhemitonic. Whole-tone scale.
Anima, con (It, kohn ah'nee'mah). With spirit.
Animato (It, ah-nee-mah'toh). Animated, with life and spirit.
Anlaufen (G). To increase in volume.
Anmutig (G, ahn'moo'tig). Graceful.
Anreissen (G). In string playing, a forceful attack.
Ansatz (G, ahn'zahts). (1) Proper adjustment of the vocal apparatus in singing; (2) embouchure in playing wind instruments. (3) In violin playing, attack.
Anschlag (G, ahn'schlag). In piano playing, touch. An ornament.
Anschwellend (G, ahn'shvel-lent). Crescendo.
Answer. In a fugue, the second statement of the subject.
Antecedent. The subject of a fugue or canon; the first phrase of a musical period.
Anthem. A choral composition with a religious text, with or without accompaniment.
Anticipation. The advancing of one or more harmonic voices or parts before the other parts.
Antico (L, ahn-tee'koh). Ancient, old.
Antienne (F). (1) Antiphon; (2) anthem.
Antiphon, antiphone (Greek). Alternate or responsive signing or chanting.
Antwort (G, ahnt'vohrt). Answer.
Anvil. Instrument made of steel bars struck with a hard wooden or metal beater.
Anwachsend (G, ahn'vahk-sent). Crescendo.
Aperto (It, ah-pair'toh). Open.

A piacere-Arpeggio

A piacere (It, ah pee-ah-che'reh). At pleasure.
A poco (It, ah poh'koh). By degrees, gradually.
A poco a poco. Little by little.
Appassionato (It, ah-pah-shee-oh-nah'toh). With intense feeling, passionately.
Appenato (It, ahp-peh-nah'toh). Distressed, suffering, grieved.
Appoggiando (It, ah-pohd-jee-ahn'doh). 'Leaning on', or supported. Full legato.
Appoggiatura (It, ah-pohd-jee-ah-too'rah). In modern usage, a strong dissonant note occurring in place of a harmonic note. Originally an ornamental note that was melodically connected with the main note that followed it.
Arabesque. A fanciful title used by some composers of the Romantic Era for pieces of a casual nature. Also used as a name for ornamental passages of a melody.
Arcato (It, ahr-kah'toh). Bowed; with a bow.
Archet, archetto, arco. A violin bow.
Archlute. A lute with two pegboxes, one for the fingered strings and one for the bass courses.
Arcicembalo (It, ahr-chee-chem-bah'loh), **arciorgano** (It, ahr-chee-or-gah'noh). Sixteenth century microtonic instruments that had six manuals with 31 keys to the octave. Others had 18 keys to the octave.
Ardente (It, ahr-den'teh). Vehement, fiery.
Ardito (It, ahr-dee'toh). Boldly, spirited.
Ardore, con (It, kohn ahr-doh'reh). With warmth, ardor.
Aria (It, ah'ree-ah). An air, tune, song. An elaborate composition for solo voice, sometimes for two voices, usually with accompaniment.
Aria buffa. A comic or humorous air.
Aribú (Also called 'lundu'). An Afro-Brazilian dance song of rural origin.
Arietta. A small aria, usually in binary form.
Arioso (It, ah-ree-oh'soh). A recitative of lyrical and expressive quality.
Armure (F). Key Signature.
Arpa (It, ahr'pah). Harp.
Arpeggiando, arpeggiato. Arpeggio.
Arpeggio (It, ahr-ped'jee-oh). Broken chord. The tones follow one another in harp style.

Arraché-Aufschnitt

Arraché (F). Forceful pizzicato.

Arrangement. The adaptation of all or part of a composition for a medium different from that for which it was originally written. Bach, Haydn, Liszt, Brahms, and other famous composers did many arrangements.

Arsis, thesis (Greek, literally 'lifting' and 'lowering'). Upbeat and downbeat.

Articulation. Distinct enunciation and clarity in musical performance, vocal and instrumental, phrasing, breathing, attack, staccato, legato.

Art song. A song of serious artistic intent, as distinct from a folk song.

As (G, ahss). The note A flat.

Asas (G, ahs'ahss). The note A double flat.

ASCAP. American Society of Composers, Authors and Publishers.

Assai (It, ah-sah'ee). Very, much.

Assez (F, ahs-say'). Enough.

Atabal. Set of three single-headed drums found in the Dominican Republic.

Atabaques. Set of three-single headed upright drums found in Brazil.

Atem (G, ah'tem). Breath.

Atempause (G, ah'tem-pou-suh). Very short rest used in instrumental performance for articulation and phrasing. Sometimes shown by an apostrophe.

A tempo (It). Return to the preceding tempo.

Atonality (adj. 'atonal'). Absence of a focal point, tonality, and harmonic resolution through intentional disregard of tonal center. Also see Twelve-tone Technique.

Attacca (It, aht-tahk'kah). Go on. Begin the next section without pausing.

Attack. The method or style of beginning a phrase.

Aubade (F, oh-bahd'). Morning music.

Audition. (1) Hearing a performance, as that of a student. (2) Faculty of hearing.

Aufgeregt (G, owf-geh-raygt'). Excited.

Aufsatz (G). (1) Tube of an organ reed pipe. (2) Crook or shank of brass instruments.

Aufschnitt (G). Mouth of an organ pipe.

Aufstrich-Auxiliary tone

Aufstrich (G). Upbow.
Auftakt (G). Upbeat.
Auftritt (G). Scene of an opera.
Aufzug (G, owf'tsook). Act of an opera.
Augmentation. Increasing the time value of the notes of a theme or melody.
Augmented intervals. Larger by one-half step than Major or Perfect intervals.
Augmented triad. Chord composed of two Major thirds.
Ausdruck (G, ows'drook). Expression.
Aushalten (G). To sustain a note.
Auslüsung (G, ows'loo-soong). The repeating mechanism of the piano (escapement).
Ausweichung (G, ows'vike-oong). Modulation.
Auszug (G, ows-tsook). Arrangement, usually for piano, of an opera, oratorio, etc.
Authentic Cadence. Cadence with the Dominant preceding the Tonic, V-I.
Autoharp. Instrument of the zither family, used mostly for accompaniment to singing.
Auxiliary tone. Tone not essential to the harmony or melody; generally a grace note a second above or below the principal note.

B

B. (1) The seventh degree of the C major scale. (2) In German B means B flat. (3) In partbooks of the 16th century B means bass.

Badinage. A dance-like piece of jocose character used as a movement in the optional group of the 18th century suites.

Bagatelle (F, bag-ah-tel'). A trifle; a short, easy piece of music.

Bagpipe. Ancient wind instrument. One or more reed pipes are attached to a windbag or bellows. One or two of the pipes, called 'chanter', have sound holes and are used for the melody; the others called 'drones' produce only one tone each and are the accompaniment.

Baguala. Argentine folk song.

Baguette (F). Drumstick. Also, the baton of the conductor and the stick of the violin bow.

Bailecito (S). Argentine folk song of two contrasting sections, the first lively, the second slower.

Baisser (F). To lower a string tuning.

Balalaika (R, bal-ah-lye-kah). Triangular guitar, popular in Russia; normally has three strings tuned in fourths. It is made in several sizes that make up a balalaika orchestra.

Balancement (F). Eighteenth century term for tremolo.

Baldamente (It, bal-dah-men'tay). Boldly.

Balg (G). Bellows of an organ.

Ballabile (It, bal-lah'bee-lay). In the style of the dance.

Ballad. A short, simple song, usually narrative. In more recent times a popular song combining narrative and romantic elements.

Ballade (F, bahl-lahd'; G, bahl-lah'deh). A type of medieval French verse in which the refrain comes at the end of the stanza. in the 19th and 20th centuries an instrumental piece of a lyrical and romantic character.

Ballad opera-Bass

Ballad opera. A popular form of 18th century opera in England consisting of spoken dialogue alternating with musical numbers taken from ballad tunes, folk songs, or famous melodies by well-known composers.

Ballata (It, bahl-lah'tah). Fourteenth century Italian verse form in which the refrain occurs at the beginning and end of the stanza.

Ballet (F, bal-lay'). Theatrical performance by a dancing group.

Ballo (It, bahl'loh). A dance or dance tune.

Bambuco (S). Colombian dance song.

Band. A group of instrumental performers playing together.

Bandola (S, bahn-doh'lah). Small guitar of Colombia with a set of 15 strings.

Bandora. 16th century stringed instrument of bass size with a characteristic scalloped body. Seven pairs of metal strings.

Bandurria (S, bahn-door'ree-ah). Spanish instrument of the guitar family.

Banjo. A stringed instrument with a long neck. The body is in the form of a shallow, one-headed drum spanned with parchment. From five to nine strings. Sometimes fretted.

Bar. Vertical line that divides the staff into measures.

Barcarole, barcarolle. Boat song of the Venetian gondoliers. Usually $\frac{6}{8}$ or $\frac{12}{8}$ time.

Bard. Medieval poet-musician, minstrel.

Bariolage (F, bah-ree-oh-lah'zh). A special effect in violin playing of quickly shifting back and forth between two or more strings.

Baritone. (1) The male voice between the bass and tenor. (2) Instruments (horn, oboe, saxophone) any size above the bass size. (3) Abbr. for Baritone Horn.

Bar line. Vertical line that divides the staff into measures.

Baroque music. Music of the period 1600–1750.

Barré (F, bar-ray'). In lute and guitar playing holding the forefinger across several or all of the strings.

Barrel organ. Mechanical organ. Tones are produced by the revolution of a cylinder.

Baryton. Baritone.

Bass. (1) The lowest of men's voices. (2) German name for the double bass. (3) The lowest and largest of any family of instruments. (4) In composition, the lowest of the parts.

33

Bassa-Bel

Bassa (It, bahs'sah). Low, deep. *8va bassa:* play the notes an octave lower.

Bass bar. In violins a strip of wood glued inside the table just beneath the G string. It supports the left foot of the bridge and equalizes vibrations.

Bass clef. F clef on the 4th line.

Basset horn. Tenor clarinet.

Basso. Bass.

Bassoon. A double reed instrument of deep pitch with a compass of three octaves; of the oboe family.

Baton (F, bah-tohn). A conductor's stick.

Battaglia. Composition in which fanfares, cries, drum rolls, and commotion of a battle are imitated.

Battement (F, baht-mahn). (1) Seventeenth century term for any ornament of an alternation of two adjacent notes, mordent, trill, vibrato. (2) Today's usage, acoustical beats.

Batterie (F, bat-tree). Battery. (1) Percussion group of the orchestra. (2) A drum roll. (3) Eighteenth century name for arpeggio, broken chord figures. (4) Playing the guitar by striking the strings.

Battuta (It, bah-too'tah). Beat. In strict time. Downbeat.

Be (G, bay). The flat sign [♭]

Beat. (1) Unit of measurement in music as indicated by the up and down movements, real or imagined, of a conductor's hand (upbeat and downbeat). (2) Seventeenth century English ornament.

Beats. An acoustical phenomenon resulting from the interference of two sound waves of slightly different frequencies.

Bebung (G, bay'boong). A vibrato sign used on the clavichord. Sign: [⁀]

Bec (F). The mouthpiece of the clarinet or recorder.

Bécarre (F, bay-car). The natural sign [♮]

Becken (G). Cymbals.

Bedächtig (G). Unhurried, deliberate.

Begleitung (G, beh-glye'toong). Accompaniment.

Behaglich (G). Comfortably, with ease.

Behende (G). Nimbly, quickly.

Beisser (G). Eighteenth century name for mordent.

Bel. Unit for measuring changes in the intensity of sound.

Bel canto-Block harmony

Bel canto (It, bell-kahn'toh). The art of beautiful song. Opposite of recitative, bravura.
Belebend, belebt (G). Brisk, animated.
Bell. (1) Bell-shaped opening of wind instruments, such as the horn or trumpet. (2) Metal percussion instrument set in vibration by a clapper inside or a hammer outside.
Bell-lyra. Glockenspiel.
Bells. Orchestral glockenspiel or the chimes.
Belly. (1) The upper side of the resonant box of violins, lutes, etc. (2) The piano soundboard.
Bémol (F), **bemolle** (It). The flat sign [♭]
Ben, bene. Well, good.
Bequadro (It, bay-kwah'droh). The natural sign [♮]
Berceuse (F, bair-suz'). Lullaby.
Bergamasca (It, bair-gah-mahs'kah). Rustic dance of Italian peasants.
Bergerette (F, bair-zhair-et'). Rustic or pastoral song; also a type of French lyrical poetry.
Beruhigt, beruhigend (G). Calm, quieting.
Bes (G, bess). B double flat [♭♭]
Beschleunigt (G). Hastened, accelerando.
Bestimmt (G, beh-shtimt'). With decision.
Betont (G, beh-tohnt'). Accented, stressed.
Bewegt (G, beh-vaygt'). Animated, agitated.
Bicinium. Sixteenth century name for a composition in two parts without accompaniment.
Binary. Two part. Binary form, two section, contrasting themes.
Bind. Tie.
Bis (L, bees). Twice, repeated. In French and Italian, request for an encore.
Bisbigliando (It, bees-beel-yahn'doh). Special effect in harp playing, a quickly repeated motion of the finger resulting in a soft tremolo.
Biscroma. Thirty-second note.
Bisdiapason. Interval of two octaves.
Bitonality. Use of two different Keys at the same time in a composition.
Blockflöte (G, blok-flut'uh). The recorder.
Block harmony. Succession of identical or similar chords.

35

Blues-Braille music notation

Blues. A genre of African American music in $\frac{4}{4}$ time, generally twelve bars long and divided into three phrases of four bars each.

Bluette. (1) Short, brilliant piece. (2) Spark, flash.

B moll (G, bay mohl′). B flat minor.

Bocca (It). Mouthpiece of a brass instrument.

Bocca chiusa (It, bok′kah kee-oo′zah). With closed mouth, humming.

Body. (1) Resonance box of a stringed instrument. (2) The part of a wind instrument remaining after the removal of mouthpiece, crooks, and bell. (3) Tube of an organ pipe above its mouth. (4) Full and sonorous tone.

Bogen (G, bo′gn). (1) Bow of a violin. (2) Slur, tie.

Bois (F, bwah). Woodwinds.

Bolero. Lively, Spanish dance in triple meter to the accompaniment of castanets.

Bombarda (It), **bombarde** (F). (1) Bass size of a shawm (oboe). (2) Organ stop, solo reed type.

Boogie woogie. Type of piano blues with a bass ostinato figure.

Bop. Type of jazz with improvised solos in a complex idiom.

Bouche (F, boosh). Mouth.

Bouche fermée (F, boosh fair-may′). With closed mouth, humming.

Bouffe (F, boof). Comic, burlesque.

Bourdon (F, boor-dawn). (1) Large pipes of the organ. (2) A drone bass such as that produced on the lower strings of the hurdy-gurdy.

Bourrée (F, boo-ray′). Seventeenth century French dance in quick duple time with one upbeat.

Boutade (F, boo-tahd′). (1) Dance or ballet in a capricious style. (2) Eighteenth century instrumental pieces of the same character.

Bow. Device made of wood and horsehair used to produce the vibrations of a stringed instrument.

Bowing. The art of using the bow, as above.

Brace. The bracket connecting two or more staffs of a musical score, or the group of staffs so connected.

Braille music notation. Method of writing music according to the principles of the Braille system for the blind.

Brass band. Group of brass instruments.
Brass instruments. Trumpet, cornet, bugle, trombone, tuba, baritone horn, euphonium.
Bratsche (G, braht-sheh). Viola.
Brautlied (G, browt-leet). Wedding song.
Bravo (It, brah'voh). Excellent, very good. Exclamation of approval used in theatres.
Bravura (It, brah-voo-rah). Spirit, skill. Requiring great dexterity and skill.
Breit (G). Broad, largo.
Breve (L, brehv). Short. In ancient times, the shortest note. Now the longest note. Equal to two whole notes.
Bridge. The part of the stringed instrument that supports the strings.
Brillante (It, breel-lahn-teh). Brilliant, showy, sparkling.
Brillenbass (G). Derogatory nickname for stereotyped accompanying figures in the manner of Alberti bass.
Brindisi (It, breen-dee'zee). Drinking song.
Brio, con (It, bree'oh). With vigor and spirit.
Brisé (F, bree-zay). Eighteenth century name for the turn. In violin playing, detached bowing.
Broderie (F). French term for coloratura. Same as auxiliary tone.
Broken chords. Chord tones sounded in succession, not together.
Broken octaves. Octaves in which the tones are sounded separately.
Brumeux (F). Misty, veiled.
Brummeisen (G). Jew's harp.
Brummstimmen (It, broom'shtim'men). Humming. Closed mouth.
Brunette (F). Seventeenth and 18th century type of French popular song.
Bruscamente (It, broo-skah-mehn'teh). Brusquely, coarsely.
Buccina (L). Old Roman brass instrument.
Buchstabenschrift (G). Letter notation.
Buffet (F). Organ case.
Buffo, buffa (It, boof-foh, boof-fah). Comic, humorous. Comic style.

Bugle-Buysine

Bugle. Instrument of copper or brass similar to the cornet. Used for military field music.
Bühne (G, boo′neh). Stage.
Bühnenfestspiel (G, boo′nehn′fehst-shpeel). Stage festival play.
Bühnenmusik (G, boo′nehn′moo-zeek). Incidental music for plays or music performed on the stage.
Burden. (1) Refrain. (2) Drone of bagpipe.
Burla, burlesca (It). Jest, playful.
Burletta (It, boor-leh′tah). Comic operetta.
Burrasca (It). Composition descriptive of a tempest or thunderstorm.
Buysine, buzine, busine (L). Trumpet of medieval times.

C

C. (1) First tone of the C scale. (2) Abbreviation for Con, Cantus, Capo, Contralto.

Cabaletta (It, kah-bah-leh′tah). Short, operatic song in popular style with rather uniform rhythm in the vocal line and accompaniment.

Caccia (It, kaht′chah). Chase, the hunt.

Cachucha (S, kah-choo′chah). Popular Spanish dance in triple time, similar to the Bolero.

Cachullapi. Ecuadorian Indian song of a single theme in fast $\frac{6}{8}$ time. Melody is usually based on a descending pentatonic (c′-a-g-f-d).

Cacophony (kah-kawf′ah-nee). Discordant, harsh sound.

Cadence. Lit, 'a falling'. (L, cado, 'I fall'). The name seems to originate from the fact that prior to 1500 the most frequent cadential motion was the descending second to the tonic. Melodic and harmonic formulas have developed for various periods of music history. Cadence has come to mean a harmonic progression that suggests a conclusion, if only a temporary one. Here are the most usual cadences of the classical and romantic periods:

Authentic   Plagal   Deceptive or Interrupted   Half

The revived interest in the use of modes in modern times has led to the use of a cadence in which the seventh degree of the scale is not raised:

Other variations of cadences are used in 20th century music, such as dissonant final chords, polytonal formations, 'contrapuntal' type cadences, etc.

Cadence. Seventeenth century name for the trill.

Cadenza (It, kah-den′dzah). A passage or section in a style of brilliant improvisation, usually near the end of a composition, where it serves as a retarding element and gives the performer a chance to exhibit his technical mastery.

Cadenzato. Rhythmical.

Caisse (F, kays′suh). Drum.

Caisse, gross. Bass drum.

Caisse, roulante. Side drum.

Calando (It, kah-lahn′doh). Gradually diminishing.

Calcando (It, kahl-kahn′doh). Pressing forward and hurrying the time.

Calliope (kahl-eye′oh-pee). An instrument of steamblown whistles played from a keyboard.

Calma, calmando, calmato (It). Quieting, tranquil.

Calore, con (It, kahn kah-law′reh). With warmth.

Cambia, cambiano (It). Direction in orchestral scores to change instruments or tuning.

Cambiata. Changed note. Nonharmonic tone.

Camera, chamber. A term applied to music of the Baroque Era composed for private performance, not church. In modern Italian usage *musica da camera* means chamber music.

Camerata (It). Sixteenth century name for small academies.
Camminando (It, kahm-mee-nahn'doh). 'Walking', flowing, moving on.
Campana (It, kahm-pah'nah). A bell.
Campanello. A small bell.
Cancel. The Natural. [♮]
Canción (S). Song.
Cancionero (S). Collection of Spanish folk songs.
Cancrizans (It, kahn-kree-tsans). Going backward, retrograde.
Canon. The strictest form of contrapuntal composition in which each voice imitates exactly the melody sung or played by the first voice.
Canonic treatment, style. Short passages written as a more or less free canon and becoming part of a larger composition.
Cantabile (It, kahn-tah'bee-leh). Singable, singing style.
Cantata. A vocal work with instrumental accompaniment consisting usually of a number of choruses, arias, recitatives, duets, etc., based on a narrative text that is lyrical, dramatic, or religious.
Cantato (It). 'Sung'.
Canticle. A sacred hymn or song. Non-metrical hymns of praise from the Bible.
Cantilena (It, kahn-tee-lay'nah). Vocal melody of a lyrical rather than a dramatic or virtuoso character.
Cantino. The highest string of lutes, viols.
Cantio sacra (L). Motet.
Cantique. Canticle.
Canto (It, kahn'toh). Song, melody, soprano.
Cantor. A singer, a chanter.
Cantus firmus (L). Melody that becomes the basis of a polyphonic composition by the addition of contrapuntal voices.
Canzona, canzone (It). Song, ballad.
Canzonet, canzonetta (It). Short songs.
Capellmeister (G). Old spelling for Kapellmeister.
Capo (It). Head, beginning.

Capotasto-Centitone

Capotasto (It). (1) The nut of stringed instruments that have fingerboards. (2) A device fastened over the fingerboard of a stringed instrument to shorten the strings uniformly and change the Key.

Cappella (It, kahp-pel'lah). Choir, orchestra. In the Middle Ages, a small chapel.

Capriccio (It, kah-prit'choh). Instrumental piece of a humorous or capricious character.

Carillon. A set of bells played from a keyboard or by a clock mechanism.

Carol. A joyous song.

Carrée (F). The double whole note or breve.

Carrure (F). The symmetrical construction of musical phrases in measures of 2, 4, 8, etc., found particularly in dances.

Cassa (It, kah'sah). Drum.

Cassation. Eighteenth century instrumental form designed for outdoor performance.

Castanets. Pair of small concave pieces of wood or ivory, attached by a cord to a dancer's thumb and forefinger and struck together with the music.

Castrato (It, kah-strah'toh). An adult male singer with soprano or alto voice.

Catch. A humorous composition, supposedly of English invention, for three or four voices. The parts are so contrived that the singers catch up each other's words, thus giving them a different sense from that of the original. The oldest catches were rounds.

Cavatina. Short solo song simpler in style than an aria. Usually no repetition.

Cédez (F, say-day). Go slower.

Celere (It, cheh'leh'reh). Rapid, swift.

Celesta. Percussion instrument of tuned steel bars connected to a keyboard.

Cello (Abbr. for *violoncello*). The bass size of the violin, tuned an octave and a fourth below it. It is about twice the length of the violin.

Cembalo (It, chem'bah-loh). Harpsichord.

Centitone. Unit for measuring intervals, exactly $1/100$ of a whole tone.

Cento (L), **centon** (F), **centone** (It). Literally 'patchwork'. The term and its derivatives, 'centonization' and 'to centonize', mean literary and musical works made up of selections from other works.

Cents. The unit of a scientific method of measuring musical intervals. It has been widely adopted in acoustics as well as in ethnomusicology. The cent is equal to $1/100$ of a half-step of the well-tempered scale. The half-step equals 100 cents, the octave contains 1200.

Cercar la nota (It, chair-kahr lah noh'tah). In vocal technic, a slight anticipation of the next note.

Ces (G, tsess). C flat.

Ceses (G, tsess'ess). C double flat.

Cetera, cetra (It). Zither, cittern.

Chaconne (F). Instrumental piece of a series of variations in slow triple time.

Chalumeau (F, shah-loo-moh'). Seventeenth century name for an early clarinet, an early oboe.

Chamber music. In a broad sense any music suited to a room or small hall. Practically, the term is most frequently applied to pieces of instrumental music in the sonata form, as trios, quartets, quintets, etc.

Chance music. See Aleatory music.

Change ringing. The ringing of bells in varying and systematic order.

Chanson (F, shahn-sohn'). A song.

Chant. General term for sacred liturgical music similar to plainsong.

Chanter. The melody pipe of the bagpipe.

Chanterelle (F, shahn-t'rel). Highest string of any instrument of the violin or lute family.

Chantey, chanty, shanty. Names for work songs of English and American sailors, sung while pulling ropes or doing work requiring concerted effort.

Character piece. Nineteenth century composition, mostly for piano or piano and one solo instrument, designed to express a definite mood or programmatic idea.

Charango. Small guitar used mainly by Indians in the Andean highlands.

Chasse (F, shass). Hunting. The hunt.

Che (It, kay). Than, that, which.
Chef (F, shehf). Leader, chief.
Chef d'orchestre (F, shehf dor-kes'tr). Conductor of an orchestra.
Chelys. Greek name for lyre, which was frequently made from a turtle shell.
Cheng. French spelling for sheng, the Chinese mouth organ.
Chest voice. Lower register of a voice.
Chevalet (F, sheh-vah-lay'). Bridge of violins.
Chevé system. System of musical notation used in France for teaching purposes. It combines the idea of the movable *do* with indicating notes by numbers. 1 to 7 represent the tones of the scale in any given Key. Lower or higher octaves are indicated by a dot under or above the numbers. A rest is indicated by 0.
Cheville (F). Peg of stringed instruments.
Chevrotement (F). Unsteadiness in singing.
Chiaramente (It). Clearly, distinctly.
Chiave (It, kee-ah'veh). Clef.
Chimes. A set of metal tubes, vertically suspended in a frame, tuned chromatically from c' to f'', and struck with one or two wooden mallets. Term is also used for carillon, glockenspiel, and various oriental bells.
Chinese block. Percussion instrument used in jazz bands; hollowed out wooden block. Played with a drumstick, it produces a dry, hollow sound.
Ching. Korean gong.
Chitarra (It, kee-tah'rah). Guitar.
Chiuso (It, kew'soh). Stopped.
Choir. A company of church singers, as opposed to a secular chorus. Term also used for instrumental groups of the orchestra.
Choir organ. Originally a small organ to accompany the choir. Now the third manual on an organ provided with stops useful for accompaniment purposes.
Choral (Adj.). Relating to the choir.
Choral, chorale (Noun). Hymn tune.
Chorale cantata (G). Cantatas in which chorale texts are used.
Chorale fantasia. Organ composition based on a chorale melody and written in a free style.

Chorale fugue. Composition usually for organ in which the initial line of a chorale melody becomes the theme of the fugue.

Chorale motet. Motet using a chorale melody.

Chorale partita (G). Chorale variations.

Chorale prelude. Composition for organ based on a chorale and designed to be played before the chorale is sung by the congregation.

Chorale variations. Variations on a chorale melody, nearly always for organ or the harpsichord, but sometimes for the lute.

Chord. The sounding together of three or more tones. Two tones are usually designated as an interval. A chord may be represented by two tones, however, with a third tone implied.

Chorlied (G). Choral song, usually without accompaniment.

Chorus. (1) Company of singers not connected with a church. (2) Music for such a group. (3) A refrain.

Chromatic. Proceeding by half-steps.

Church modes. See Modes.

Ciaccona (It, chahk-koh′nah). Chaconne.

Cibell, cebell. Seventeenth century name for gavotte.

Cimbalom. Large dulcimer.

Cimbasso (It). Narrow bore tuba in B flat.

Cinelli (It, chee-nehl′lee). Cymbals.

Ciphering. The continued sounding of the pipes of an organ due to a mechanical defect.

Circle of fifths. The circular arrangement of Major and minor Keys in an order of ascending fifths showing that after twelve such steps the initial Key is reached again.
See page 7.

Cis (G, tsiss). C sharp.

Cisis (G, tsiss′iss). C double sharp.

Cister, cistre, cither, citole, cittern. Lute or guitar.

Clarinet. Rich, full-toned tubular instrument of wood, ebonite, or metal. Single reed played by means of holes and keys. Three-octave range.

Clarinet family. Large group of single-reed woodwind instruments.

Clarino (It, klah-ree′noh). (1) High register of the clarinet. (2) Virtuoso method of trumpet playing in the 17th century.

Clarion. Small English trumpet.
Clarone. Bass clarinet.
Clarsech, clairseach. Irish harp.
Clavecin, clavessin. Harpsichord.
Clavichord. Stringed keyboard instrument, forerunner of the pianoforte. Tone is soft, but pleasing. When a key is depressed, its tangent (a brass blade driven into the back end of the key) strikes a pair of strings.
Clavier. French term for keyboard (pronounced klah-vee-ay; in English usage, klah-vee'air). German term (klah'veer) used in the Baroque period as a designation for keyboard instruments such as the harpsichord, clavichord, and organ.
Clef. A sign at the beginning of a staff to indicate the pitch of the notes.
Cloche (F, klawsh). A bell.
Close. Cadence.
Close harmony. Notes or parts as close together as possible.
Coda. Lit. 'tail'. Ending section or passage.
Codetta. A short coda. In the exposition of a fugue, any short transitional section between two entries of the subject.
Col arco (It). With a bow (after *pizzicato*).
Col legno (It). In violin playing, striking the strings with the bow-stick instead of playing with the hair.
Coll' ottava (It). At the octave. Indication to duplicate the written notes at the upper octave.
Coll' ottava bassa. Direction to duplicate the written notes as the lower octave.
Coloratura (It, koh-loh-rah-too'rah). Rapid passage, run, trill or similar virtuoso-like material in vocal music. Also used for instrumental ornaments.
Come (It, koh'meh). As, like.
Come prima (It). As before, as at first.
Come sopra (It). As above.
Come sta (It). As its stands, as written.
Comic opera. General name for an opera or other dramatic work with a mixture of music of a light or sentimental nature, with comic elements and a happy ending.
Comma, schisma. Minute differences in pitch that occur in the calculation of intervals if the same note is obtained through

Common chord-Conjunct

different combinations of octaves, Perfect fifths, and pure Major thirds.
Common chord. Major or minor triad.
Common time. $\frac{4}{4}$ meter.
Commodo (It, koh-moh′doh). Comfortable.
Compass. The range of a voice or instrument.
Composition. Any musical work. The art of creating or putting together musical works.
Compound binary form. Sonata form.
Compound interval. One which exceeds the extent of an octave, as a 9th, 10th, etc.
Compound stop. Mixture stop on the organ.
Compound meters. Those which include or exceed six parts in a measure and contain two or more principal accents, as $\frac{6}{4}$, $\frac{6}{8}$, $\frac{9}{8}$, $\frac{12}{8}$.
Con (L). With.
Concert. A public performance of music.
Concertant (F); **concertante** (I). A piece for two or more solo instruments or voices with orchestral accompaniment in which each solo part is in turn brought into prominence.
Concertina. A small instrument similar to the accordion, the sound boxes being hexagonal in shape instead of oblong.
Concertmaster. First violinist of the orchestra. Usually plays the solo violin passages and may substitute for the conductor.
Concerto. Composition for orchestra and a solo instrument in modified sonata form.
Concerto grosso. Composition using a small group of solo instruments with an orchestra.
Concert pitch. Term used for standard international pitch, a=440 vibrations per second.
Concitato (It, kohn-chee-tah′toh). Agitated.
Concord, discord. Sounds that are pleasing to the ear (triads, seventh chords, and other pleasing chords); discord means deliberately harsh and unpleasant sounds.
Conducting. Leading or directing a performing group.
Conductor. Leader or director of an orchestra or chorus.
Conductor's part. Abbreviated score of orchestral works.
Conjunct. Successive degrees of a scale, an interval of a second.

Consecutive intervals–Cor Anglais

Consecutive intervals. Intervals of the same kind following one another in immediate succession.

Consequent. The answer. (1) A musical phrase following a similar one. (2) Antecedent and consequent stand for the question and answer relationship of melodic phrases. (3) Subject and answer in a canon or fugue.

Conservatory. A school especially for music training.

Console. That part of the organ from which the player controls the instrument, including the keyboards, pedals, stops, case, etc. In modern organs, it is often placed apart from the rest of the organ, the sole connection being the electrical wiring.

Consonance. Generally, intervals that are harmonious and "pleasing." However, there is no absolute agreement as to which intervals or chords are consonant and which are dissonant. Traditionally, the Major and minor thirds, the Perfect fourths and fifths, the Major and minor sixth, and the Perfect octave are classed as consonant.

Consort. Seventeenth century English term for instrumental chamber ensembles or for music written for them.

Contano (It, kohn-tah'noh). Rest. When certain parts have rests for the time being while other parts continue.

Contemporary music. Present-day music.

Continuo (It, kohn-tee'noo-oh). The bass line of a composition marked with figures to indicate the harmonies to be played on a keyboard instrument.

Contra (L, It). 'Against'. Prefixed to names of instruments, 'an octave below'.

Contrabass. Double bass of the string family.

Contrabassoon. Deepest instrument of the bassoon family.

Contrafagotto. Double bassoon.

Contralto. Lowest female voice.

Contrappunto. Counterpoint.

Contrapuntal. In the style of counterpoint.

Contrary motion. Parts moving in the opposite direction, one rising as the other falls.

Coperto (It, koh-payr'toh). Covered, muffled.

Copla (S). Couplet or stanza of Spanish songs.

Copyright, musical. See page 148.

Cor (F, kor). Horn.

Cor Anglais. English horn.

Coranto-Courante

Coranto (It, koh-rahn′toh). Courante.
Corda (It). A string. *Una corda* in piano music means 'one string': i.e., press the left pedal so that only one string sounds. *Tre corda* means to release the left pedal so that all three strings sound again. In violin, *corda vuota* means 'open string'.
Corista (It). Orchestral pitch, tuning fork.
Cornemuse (It). Bagpipe.
Cornet. Small brass wind instrument with three valves, similar to the trumpet.
Corno. Horn.
Cornu. Ancient Roman horn.
Coro (It). A choir, chorus.
Corona (It). [⌢] The pause or hold.
Corrente (It). Courante.
Cortège. Composition in the character of a solemn procession or a triumphal march.
Coulé (F, koo-lay′). French 18th century ornament in the character of an appoggiatura.
Coulisse (F). The slide of a trombone or slide trumpet.
Count. Beat or pulse of measure.
Counter. Part sung or played against another. Contrasting part.
Counterexposition. Name sometimes given to the second exposition of a fugue.
Counterfugue. Fugue in which the answer is the inverted form of the subject.
Counterpoint. 'Note against note' or 'melody against melody'. Before the invention of notes, the various sounds were expressed by points. Counterpoint is the support of melody by melody rather than by chords (harmony). The texture is horizontal.
Counter subject. The second division in a fugue coming against the answer in the second voice.
Coup d'archet (F, koo dahr-shay). Bow stroke.
Coup de langue (F, koo duh lahng′). Tonguing.
Coupler. Mechanical device on organs and harpsichords that connects two or more manuals so that when one is played on, the other is combined with it.
Couplet. Two successive lines forming a pair.
Courante (F, koo-rahn′t). Running dance.

Course-Czardas

Course. In stringed instruments, especially those of the lute family, a group of strings tuned in unison or an octave apart and plucked at the same time to obtain more volume.

Covered fifths, octaves. Same as hidden fifths, octaves.

Cow bells. Instruments similar in shape and sound to bells worn by cows in the Alps, but without the clappers. Struck with a drumstick.

Crash cymbal. Single cymbal hung from a cord and struck with a drumstick.

Crescendo (It, kreh-shen'doh). Gradually becoming louder, stronger in volume.

Crescent. A Turkish instrument made of small bells hung on an inverted crescent.

Cross relation. A chord progression in which a note in one part in the first chord is followed by a chromatic alteration of the same note in another part in the second chord. Also the simultaneous sounding in a single chord of a note and its chromatic alteration.

Crotchet. Quarter note.

Crwth (krooth). Ancient Welsh or Irish harp played with a bow.

Csárdás (Hun, chahr'dahsh). Hungarian dance.

Cue. A short passage taken from another part and printed in small notes to serve as a guide for the entrance of the player or singer after a long rest.

Cycle. In musical acoustics, a double vibration. Also, various systems of equal temperament.

Cyclic, cyclical. Term for any musical form made up of several complete forms, movements, or compositions placed in contrast with each other. Sonata, cantata, suite, symphony, etc.

Cymbals. Percussion instrument consisting of two metal plates that are struck together.

Czardas. Alternate spelling for csárdás.

D

D. Second degree of the C Major scale. Abbr. For 'Da', or 'Dal', as D. S., 'Dal Segno': D. C., 'Da Capo'.
Da (It, dah). By, from, for, through.
Da capo (It, dah kah′poh). From the beginning. Indication that a piece is to be repeated from the beginning to the end or to a place marked *Fine.*
Dal (It, dahl). From the, by the, of the.
Dal segno (It, dahl say-nyoh). From the sign.
Damper. In pianos and harpsichords, the part of the mechanism that stops the vibration of the string, therefore the sound, at the moment the key is released.
Damper pedal. Pedal of the pianoforte that lifts the dampers from the strings and allows them to vibrate freely.
Début (F, day-bew′). First appearance.
Deceptive cadence. See Cadence.
Decibel. Unit for measuring changes in the intensity of sound.
Decima (L, des′ee-mah). A tenth. Interval of ten degrees in a diatonic scale.
Deciso (t, day-chee′zoh). Decided, bold.
Decrescendo (It, day-kreh-shen′doh). Softer. Gradually diminishing in amount of tone.
Decuplet. Group of ten equal notes played in the time of eight notes of like value, or to four notes of the next highest value. Marked by a slur and 10.
Degree. The step between two notes, each line and space of the staff. See page 13.
Dehors, en (F, anh deh-or′). With emphasis.
Del, della (It). Of the.
Demi (F, deh-mee). Half.
Demisemiquaver. Thirty-second note.
Derb (G, dairb). Robust, rough.
Des (G, dess). D flat.

Descant -Diminished interval

Descant (L). The addition of a part or parts to a subject. Forerunner of modern counterpoint, this art grew out of the still earlier art of organum. In the latter, the parts ran in parallel motion, but in descant, oblique and contrary motion of parts began to appear as early as the 11th or 12th century. In modern hymn singing, an obbligato part that soars above the tune is called a descant.

Deses (G, dehs'ehs). D double flat.

Détaché (F, day-tah-shay'). In violin playing, detached, staccato.

Detonieren (G). To sing off pitch, waver.

Deutlich (G). Clear, distinct.

Deux (F, doo). Two.

Development. The working out or elaboration of a theme by making new combinations of its figures and phrases. The development section in sonata form.

Dezime (G). Interval of the 10th.

Di (It, dee). Of, from, to, by.

Dia (Greek). Through, throughout.

Diabolus in musica (L). Late medieval nickname for the tritone, which in music theory was regarded as the 'most dangerous' interval.

Diacisma, diaschisma. A microtonic interval in medieval theory.

Diapason. (1) In Greek and medieval theory, the interval that includes all the tones, the octave. (2) Main foundation stop of the organ.

Diatonic. By, through, with, within, or embracing the tones of the standard Major or minor scale to the exclusion of any chromatic tones.

Dice music. See Aleatory music.

Dièse (F, dee-ez'). The note A sharp.

Diferencia (S). Sixteenth century name for variation.

Digitone. A system of music notation developed in the United States in the late 20th century that uses numerals for the 12 tones of the octave and metric notation for rhythm.

Diluendo (It, dee-loo-ehn'doh). Growing softer.

Diminished interval. Intervals one-half step smaller than Perfect or minor intervals.

Diminished chords-Dodecaphonic

Diminished chords. Chords that have a diminished interval between their highest and lowest notes.
Diminuendo (It, dee-mee-noo-en'doh). Abbr. dim. Gradually softer.
Diminution. Imitation of a given subject or theme in notes of shorter duration. Decreasing the time value.
Di molto (It, dee mohl'toh). Very, extremely.
Direct. The sign [⤳] set at the end of a staff to show the position of the first note of the next staff.
Dirge. A vocal or instrumental composition designed to be performed at a funeral or in commemoration of the dead.
Dis (G, diss). D sharp.
Discant (us). See Descant.
Discord. A dissonant or inharmonious combination of sounds. In strict harmony, it must be resolved in order to satisfy the ear.
Disinvolto (It, dee-zeen-vohl'toh). Jaunty, easy, unconstrained.
Disis (G, diss'iss). D double sharp.
Disjunct motion. Progressing by skips.
Disposition. The arrangement of stops, manuals, pedals, couplers, etc., of an organ.
Dissonance. See discord.
Dital (dit'l). A key that when pressed by the finger or thumb raises the pitch of a guitar or lute one half step.
Dital harp. A guitar-shaped lute with 12 or 18 strings, each having a dital to raise its pitch one half step.
Ditonus (L, dye-toh-nuhs). Medieval name for the Major third.
Divertimento (It, dee-vair-tee-mehn'toh). (1) Short, light composition written primarily for entertainment. (2) A fugal episode.
Divertissement (F, dee-vair-tees-mahn'). An entertainment in the form of a ballet, with or without songs, included in an opera or play for the sake of variety.
Divisi (It, dee-vee'zee). Divided, separated. Indicates that two parts written on one staff are to be played by two groups of players.
Do, doh. Syllable applied to the first note of a scale. The keynote.
Dodecaphonic. Pertaining to twelve-tone technique.

Dodecuple scale-Double fugue

Dodecuple scale. The chromatic scale in its modern interpretation as used in the twelve-tone technique.

Dodecuplet. A group of 12 equal notes performed in the time of 8 notes of the same value.

Doigté (F, dwah-tay′). Fingering.

Dolce (It, dohl′cheh). Sweetly, softly.

Dolcian, dolciana, dolciano. An early kind of bassoon, formerly used as a tenor to the oboe.

Dolendo, dolent, dolente (It). Sorrowful.

Dominant. The fifth degree of a Major or minor scale.

Dominant chord. Triad built on the dominant degree of the scale.

Dominant seventh chord. Dominant triad with the addition of a minor seventh from the bass (G-B-D-F).

Dombra. Central Asian long-necked lute; a forerunner of the Russian balalaika.

Donnermachine (G). Thunder machine.

Dopo (It, doh′poh). After.

Doppel (G, dohp′pel). Double.

Dorian. See Modes.

Dot. (1) The mark following a note that increases that note's value one-half. (2) The mark over or under a note that means staccato.

Double. (1) Old name for variation. (2) To add the higher or lower octave.

Double bar. Two vertical lines drawn through the staff at the end of a section, movement, or piece.

Double bass. Largest and deepest-toned instrument of the violin family.

Double chorus. Use of two choruses in alternation.

Double concerto. Concerto for two instruments and orchestra.

Double corde. Double stop.

Double counterpoint. A passage in which the lower part may become the higher part, or the higher the lower.

Double croche. Sixteenth note.

Double dot. Two dots that increase the value of the note they follow by three-fourths of its original value.

Double flat [♭♭] Lowers the tone one whole step.

Double fugue. A fugue with two subjects.

Double note-Dulcimer

Double note. Breve. A note that is twice the length of a whole note.

Double octave. The interval of a 15th or two octaves.

Double quartet. A composition for eight voices or instruments.

Double reed. Two pieces of cane joined together. A free reed.

Double sharp. [x] Raises the tone one whole step.

Double stem. A note is stemmed up and down when two voice parts written on one staff sound the same note in unison.

Double stop. The playing of two or more tones at the same time on the violin and similar instruments.

Double tonguing. Technic used by flute and brass instrument players to articulate fast tones.

Doucement (F, doos-mahn). Softly, sweetly.

Douloureux (F). Sorrowful.

Downbeat. The downward motion of the conductor's hand; the primary beat.

Down bow. [⊓] The downward stroke of the bow in violin playing.

Dramatic music. Music written for a drama.

Drängend (G, drehng'ent). Pressing on.

Drei (G, dry). Three.

Dreifach (G, dry-fakh). Triple.

Dreiklang (G). Triad.

Dreitaktig (G). In phrases of three measures.

Droit (F, drwah). Right. *Main droite,* right hand.

Drone. Low pipes of the bagpipe that sound only one pitch.

Drone bass. Long, sustained tones, usually in the lowest part.

Drum. Percussion instrument. Generic name for instruments with a skin stretched over a frame or vessel and struck with the hands or sticks. Same as membranophones.

Dudelsack (G). Bagpipe.

Due (It, doo'eh). Two. *Due corde,* two strings. In violin music, indicates that the same tone is sounded on two strings.

Duet. Composition for two voices or two instruments.

Dulciana. Organ stop.

Dulcimer. Old stringed instrument having wire strings stretched over a sounding board or resonance box, and struck with mallets or hammers. Forerunner of the pianoforte.

Dulcitone-Dynamics

Dulcitone. Kind of celesta with tuning forks instead of steel plates.
Dumka (Polish, doom'kah). Folk ballad of a melancholy character.
Duo. Duet.
Duodezime (G), **duodecima** (It). Interval of the twelfth.
Duole (G), **duolet** (F). Duplet.
Duple. Double. *Duple rhythm,* two beats to a measure.
Duplet. Group of two notes played in the time of three notes of the same value.
Dur (G, door). Major.
Duramente (It, doo-rah-mehn'teh). Harshly.
Durezza (It, doo-reht'sah). Harshly.
Dux, comes (L). The statement and answer of the theme in imitative composition such as canons and fugues.
Dynamics. The varying and contrasting degrees of intensity or loudness in musical tones.

E

E. The third degree of the C Major scale.
Ear training. An important field of instruction designed to teach the student to recognize and write down musical sounds and rhythms.
Ebollimento, ebollizione. Sudden expression of passion.
Échappement (F). Escapement of the piano.
Echegiatta. Echo effects.
Échelette (F). Xylophone.
Échelle (F). Scale.
Echo, eco. Repetition or imitation of a previous passage with less volume than before.
Écossaise. Lively dance in $\frac{2}{4}$ time.
Eguale (It, eh-gwah′leh). Equal, alike.
Eighth. An octave.
Eilend (G, eye lent). To hasten.
Ein, Eins, Eine (G). One.
Einfach (G). Simple, plain.
Eingang (G). Introduction.
Einhalt (G). A pause.
Einheit (G). Unity.
Einigkeit (G). Concord, harmony.
Einklang (G). Unison, consonance.
Einlage (G). Interpolation, insertion.
Einleitung (G). Introduction.
Einsatz (G). (1) An attack. (2) Entrance of a part.
Einstimmig (G). Monophonic.
Eintritt (G). Entrance.
Eis (G, ay′iss). E sharp.
Eisis (G, ay′iss-iss). E double sharp.
Eisteddfod (Welsh, eye-stedh′vohd). A Welsh gathering, featuring competitions in music and poetry.
Élargissent (F). Broadening in speed.

Electronic instruments-English Suites

Electronic instruments. Term for instruments in which the tone is produced, modified, or amplified by electronic circuits. Electronic instruments may be divided into three groups: (1) the tone is produced or generated by electronic circuits; (2) tone is produced by strings or reeds and amplified; (3) devices used by the composer in the creation of music; computers, synthesizers.

Electronic music. Music made by producing, amplifying, modifying, and recording sound. These sounds are then reproduced by electronic means. Traditionally, electronic music has meant sounds created exclusively by electronic means as opposed to that made by recording sounds that already exist. However, some composers combine both of these elements.

Electropneumatic action. A system of key action in organs in which the pipe valves in the wind chest are opened by pneumatic motors that are actuated by electrical impulses from the keys.

Elegy, elegie. Musical work of melancholy character.

Embellishment. Ornament.

Embouchure (F, ahm-boo-shur'). The mouthpiece of a wind instrument. Also the use of the lips and tongue in playing the instrument.

Emfindung, mit (G). With feeling.

Empressé (F). Hurrying.

Ému (F). With emotion, feeling.

Enchaînement (F). Voice-leading, proper connection of chords and/or parts.

Enchaînez (F, ahn-shnen-ay'). Go on directly.

Enclume (F). Anvil.

Encore (F, ahn'kohr'). Lit., 'again'. The repetition of a piece, or an extra piece played in response to applause by the audience.

Energico (It, aye-nair'jee-koh). With energy, decision.

Engführung (G). Stretto of fugues.

English flute. Eighteenth century name for the recorder.

English Suites. Six suites for the harpsichord composed by J. S. Bach.

Enharmonic-Éteint

Enharmonic. (1) Descriptive of tones that are the same degree of the scale, but are named and written differently. (2) In Greek music, a tonality including quarter tones.
Ensemble (F, 'together'). A group of musicians performing together. Refers to balance, unification in performance.
Entr'acte (F, ahn-trakht'). An interval between acts, or the music performed during the interval.
Entrada (S), entrata (It). Prelude or short introduction.
Entrée (F, ahn-tray'). (1) Orchestral overture to a ballet. (2) Division in a ballet somewhat like a scene in an opera.
Entry. Entrance of the theme in a fugue.
Entschieden, entschlossen (G). Resolutely.
Épinette (F, ay-pee-net'). Spinet, harpsichord.
Episode. An incidental narrative or digression not founded on the principal theme.
Equale (It, ay-kwal'lay). Composition for equal voices (all male or all female), or for equal instruments.
Equal temperament. The tuning of keyboard instruments so that all half-steps are equal.
Ergriffen (G, air-greef'n). Deeply moved.
Erlöschend (G). Fading away.
Ermattend (G). Tiring, weakening.
Ernst, ernsthaft (G). Serious.
Erotic, eroticon. Amorous composition, love song.
Ersterbend (G, air-shtair'bend). Fading away.
Es (G, ehss). E flat.
Esercizio (It, eh-zair-chee'tsee-oh). Exercise.
Eses (G, ehss'ehss). E double flat.
Espinette (F). Type of harpsichord, 16th cent.
Espressivo (It, eh-sprehs-see'voh). With expression.
Esquinazo (S). In Chile, serenade usually sung at Christmas or on special occasions.
Estampe, estampida, istanpitta, stampita. Names of an important instrumental form of the 13th and 14 centuries. From 4 to 7 sections were repeated with different endings.
Estilo. Argentine song of two sections, the first in a slow duple meter and the second in fast triple meter.
Estinto (It, ehs-teen'toh). Dying away in time and in volume.
Et (L). And.
Éteint (F, eh-taynt'). Barely audible.

59

Ethnomusicology-Expressive organ

Ethnomusicology. The study of all kinds of music, particularly from an anthropological or cultural perspective.

Étouffé (F, ay-too-fay'). Muted, damped.

Étude (F, ay-tood'). Study, exercise. A composition devoted to some aspect of technic.

Euphonium. Brass instrument similar to the baritone horn, but with a larger bore.

Evangelium (G). Gospel.

Exercise. Short piece for the improvement of the technic of the performer.

Exposition. In sonata form, the first section containing the statement of the themes. In a fugue, the first and subsequent sections that include the imitation of the theme.

Expression. The quality in musical performance which appeals to one's feelings, emotions, taste, and judgment.

Expressionism. Term borrowed from the visual arts and applied to music written in an introspective and subjective style, as in the works of early 20th century composers such as Schoenberg, Berg, Webern, and in some works, Krenek and Hindemith.

Expressive organ. Harmonium.

F

F. The fourth degree of the C major scale. In lower case, '*f*' means forte, '*ff*', fortissimo.
Fa. Name of syllable of fourth degree of scale.
Fagott (G, fah-gawt'). Bassoon.
Fagotto (It, fah-goh'toh). Bassoon.
Falsa (S, Port). Dissonance.
False. False, deceptive cadence. *False fifth (triad),* diminished fifth. False, cross relation.
Falsetto. False or artificial male voice that lies above the natural vocal range.
Fancy. A type of 16th and 17th century music written for instrumental ensemble.
Fandango. Spanish dance in triple time danced by a couple to the accompaniment of a guitar and castanets.
Fanfare. Short tune for trumpets or hunting horns.
Fantasia, fantasie, phantasie. Compositions in free style.
Farce. In plays and operas, light comedy or burlesque.
Fastoso (It, fah-stoh'soh). Pompous.
F clef. [𝄢] Bass clef.
Feeders. Small bellows used to supply the large bellows of an organ with wind.
Feierlich (G, fy'her-likh). Festive, solemn.
Feminine cadence. Cadence ending on a weak beat.
Fermata (It, fehr-mah'tah). [⌢] Hold, pause. Also pedal point in Italian.
Ferne (G, fehr'nuh). As from a distance.
Fes (G, fehss). F flat.
Festival. A series of performances.
Festive. Merry, joyous, gay.
Festoso (It, fehs-toh'zoh). Festive.
F-holes. The sound holes on a violin, etc.
Fiato (It, fee-ah'toh). Breath.
Fiddle. Colloquial name for the violin and for instruments that resemble it.

61

Fiero-Flautato

Fiero (It, fee-ay′roh). High-spirited, bold.
Fife. Small, shrill-toned flute with six to eight finger-holes and without keys.
Fifteenth. (1) Interval measuring fifteen diatonic degrees. (2) Organ stop sounding two octaves above the normal.
Fifth. Interval of five diatonic degrees.
Figuration. Consistent use of the same melodic or harmonic figure.
Figure. A distinct group of notes, a motif.
Figured bass. A bass with numerals placed over or under the notes to indicate harmony.
Figured chorale. A setting of a chorale in which a certain figure is used throughout.
Figured melody. Florid, ornamented melody.
Finale (It, fee-nah′lay). Final, concluding. (1) The last movement of a sonata or symphony. (2) Closing numbers of an opera or an oratorio.
Fine (It, fee′nay). The end.
Fingerboard. In stringed instruments, a long strip of hardwood fixed to the neck over which the strings are stretched.
Fingering. Directions for use of the fingers in playing instruments, or the fingering itself.
Fioritura (It). Embellishment, ornament.
Fis (G, fiss). F sharp.
Fistelstimme (G). Falsetto.
Fisis (G, fiss′iss). F double sharp.
Fixed Do. The tone C and all its chromatic derivatives are called *Do,* regardless of the Key or harmony in which they may appear.
Fixed syllables. Vocal syllables that do not change with the Key.
Flageolet (F, flah-zhee-oh-lay′). Whistle flute.
Flamenco. Spanish gypsy style of song, dance.
Flat [♭] Sign which means to lower the pitch of a note one-half step.
Flat, double [♭♭] Sign which means to lower the pitch of a note one whole step.
Flautato (It, flou-tah′toh). A direction in violin playing to play near the fingerboard in order to produce a somewhat "flutey" tone.

Flautino (It). A small flute.
Flauto. Flute. Until the middle of the 18th century, *flauto* meant the recorder.
Flauto piccolo. Small recorder.
Flaviol. Small Spanish flute.
Flebile (It, fleh'bee-lay). Mournful.
Fliessend(er) (G). Flowing, more flowing.
Florid. Embellished, ornamental.
Flott (G). Briskly, without hesitation.
Flourish. (1) Fanfare or trumpet call. (2) Showy passage, often added by the performer.
Flügel (G). Grand piano.
Flügelhorn. Brass instrument similar to the cornet, but larger.
Flüssig (G). Flowing.
Flute. Wind instrument, generally made of wood or metal. The modern flute is a cylindrical tube closed at the upper end. At this end is a side hole across which the player blows, making the column of air vibrate inside the tube. A direct flute is blown from the end like a whistle.
Folk music, folk song. Music and tradition of communities in contrast to art music, the work of musically trained composers. Often passed on aurally, often modified as it goes.
Foot. Unit of measure in organ pipes. Any stop sounding its natural pitch is called *8 foot;* an octave higher, *4 foot;* two octaves higher, *2 foot;* an octave lower, *16 foot.*
Form. In music, as in the other arts, the shape and order in which a piece of music is composed.
Forte (It, fohr'teh). Abbr. [*f*] Loud.
Forte-piano. Abbr. [*fp*] Loud followed by soft.
Fortissimo (It, fohr-tees'see-moh). Abbr. [*ff*] Very loud.
Fortspinnung (G). The process of continuation, development, or working out of material, in contrast to repetition.
Forzando (It, fohr-tsahn'doh). [*sfz*] With force, energy, accent.
Foundation stops. Unison and octave sounding ranks of the organ, especially of the diapason chorus.
Fourth. Interval of four diatonic degrees.
Fourth chord. Chord built by fourths.
Frauenchor (G, frow-ehn-kohr). Women's chorus.
Frei (G, fry). Free, with freedom.

Freistimmigkeit-Furioso

Freistimmigkeit (G). Term sometimes translated as 'free voice-leading', for a style in which there is no strict number of parts. Voices are free to enter or drop out, and chordal elements also occur. Most appropriate for keyboard instruments.

French harp. Mouth organ.

French horn. Orchestral instrument of brass with a funnel-shaped mouthpiece and a narrow conical bore wound into a spiral and ending in a large, flaring bell.

Frequency. Speed of vibrations.

Fret. Narrow ridge of wood, metal, or ivory fitted to the fingerboard of a stringed instrument to aid in the stopping of the strings.

Frettoloso. Hurried.

Freudig (G, froy'digh). Joyous.

Frog. Slightly raised ridge fastened to the upper end of the neck of instruments of the violin family. Raises the strings over the fingerboard.

Fröhlich (G). Joyful.

Fuga (It, foo'gah). Fugue.

Fugato. Passage in fugal style that is part of a composition. Often occurs in the development section of symphonies, sonatas, and quartets.

Fughetta (It, foo-geht'tah). Short fugue.

Fugue. A contrapuntal composition in two or more parts (voices), built on a subject that is introduced at the beginning in imitation and recurs frequently throughout the work. Most fugues include a subject, the answer, a countersubject, and a stretto. Episodes and a coda are often added.

Fundamental. The lowest tone, root of the chord. First harmonic.

Fuoco, con (It, kohn fwoh'koh). With fire.

Furioso (It, foo-ree-oh'soh). Furiously, wildly.

G

G. The fifth degree of the C major scale.
Gagaku. Orchestral music of the Japanese court, still much like its 8th century adaptation from continental Asia.
Gallant style. Light, elegant style of the Rococo Period, 18th century.
Galliard, gaillarde, gagliarda, gallarda. Rollicking 16th century dance.
Galop. Lively round dance in $\frac{2}{4}$ time.
Gamba (It, gahm-bah). Viola da gamba.
Gambang. Indonesian idiophone made of a number of wooden, bamboo, or metal bars resting on a large trough resonator.
Gamelan. Indonesian orchestra.
Gamut. Scale or range.
Ganz (G). Whole, entire.
Ganze Note, ganze Pause (G, gahnts'eh not'uh, pow'zuh). Whole note, whole note rest.
Ganzschluss (G). Full cadence.
Ganzton (G, gahnts'tohn). Whole tone.
Ganztonleiter (G). Whole tone scale.
Gapped scale. Scale that is derived from a more complete system of tones by leaving some of them out. The pentatonic scale is a gapped scale of the diatonic system, which in turn could be considered a gapped scale of the chromatic system. Most of the scales of Asian music are gapped scales, since the tones actually used in the music are only a small selection from a more complete system.
Garbato (It, gahr-bah'toh). Graceful, elegant.
Gassenhauer (G). In the 16th century, term for popular song. In present German usage, a vulgar street song.
Gathering note. The tone sounded by the organist to give the correct pitch for the singing of a hymn.
Gauche (F, gohsh). Left.
Guadioso (It, gow-dee-oh'soh). Joyous.

Gavotte-Generalpause

Gavotte. Seventeenth century French dance in $\frac{4}{4}$ time, usually beginning on an up-beat of two quarter notes, with phrases ending in the middle of the measure.
G clef. [𝄞] Treble clef.
Gebrauchsmusik (G). Music for use, 'utility music', music for amateur or home use.
Gebrochener Akkord (G). Broken chord.
Gebunden (G). Legato.
Gedackt, gedeckt (G). Stopped.
Gedämpft (G, geh-dempft'). Muted, muffled.
Gedehnt (G, geh-daynt'). Stretched out, slow.
Gefühl (G, geh-feel'). Sentiment, expression.
Gegenbewegung (G). Contrary motion between two voices. Also used as a synonym of inversion of a subject.
Gegenfuge (G, gay'-gehn-foo'guh). Counterfugue.
Gegensatz (G, gay'gehn-zatz). Contrast.
Gegenthema (G, gay'gehn-tay-mah). Countersubject of a fugue or the second theme of a sonata movement.
Gehalten (G, geh-hahlt'n). Held out, sustained.
Gehend (G, gay'end). Andante, moving.
Geige (G, gy'guh). Violin.
Geistlich (G, gyst'likh). Religious, spiritual.
Gekkin. A Japanese lute.
Gekoppelt (G, geh-kop'pehlt). Coupled.
Gelassen (G, geh-lass'n). Calm, placid.
Geläufigkeit (G, geh-loyf'fig-kyt). Technical fluency.
Gemächlich (G, geh-mekh'likh). Comfortable, leisurely.
Gemässigt (G, geh-mehss-ikt). Moderate.
Gemeindelied (G, geh-mine'duh-leet). Congregational hymn, chorale.
Gemendo (It, jay-mehn'doh). Lamenting.
Gemessen (G, geh-mehs'sehn). Restrained.
Gemischte Stimmen (G, geh-mish'tuh shtim'mehn). Mixed voices.
Gendèr (jehn'dr). Javanese metallophone made of thin bronze slabs over resonating bamboo tubes.
Generalbass (G). Thoroughbass.
Generalpause (G). Abbr. G.P. Rest for the entire orchestra coming unexpectedly after a climactic passage.

Generalprobe-Gleichmässig

Generalprobe (G). Dress rehearsal of orchestra concerts, usually open to the public.
German flute. An 18th century name for the transverse flute.
Ges (G, gehss). G flat.
Gesamtausgabe (G, geh-zahmpt'ows'gah-buh). Complete edition.
Gesang (G, geh-zahng'). Song.
Gesangbuch (G, geh-zahng'bookh). Hymnal.
Gesangvoll (G, geh-zahng'fohl). Songlike. Cantabile.
Geschick (G, geh-shikh). Skill, dexterity.
Geschleift (G, geh-shlyft). Slurred, legato.
Geschwind (G, geh-shvint'). Quick, nimble.
Geses (G, gehss'ehss). G double flat.
Gesteigert (G, geh-shty'gehrt). Increased.
Gestopft (G, geh-shtohpft'). Stopped notes of the horn.
Gestossen (G, geh-stohs'sehn). Separated, detached.
Geteilt (G, geh-tile-t). Divided.
Getragen (G, geh-trah'gn). Sustained, slow.
Ghironda (It, gee-rohn'dah). Hurdy gurdy.
Gigelira (It, jee-jeh-lee'rah). Xylophone.
Giga (It, jee'gah), **gigue** (F, zheeg), **gige** (G, gee'guh). Jig, lively dance.
Giocoso (It, jee-oh-koh'soh). Humorous, playful.
Gioioso (It, joh-yoh'soh). Joyful, cheerful.
Giro (It, jee'roh). Turn.
Gis (G, giss). G sharp.
Gisis (G, giss'iss). G double sharp.
Gitana, alla (It, ahl'lah jee-tah'nah). Gypsy style.
Giusto (It, joos'toh). Right, just. *Tempo giusto,* fitting or strict tempo.
Glass harmonica. Invented by Benjamin Franklin in 1763, the instrument resembles a spinet. Instead of keys, there is a row of glass bowls of various sizes, fixed on their sides on a spindle. The spindle is revolved into a trough of water by a treadle operated by the player's foot. The sounds are produced by rubbing the fingers against the wet glass. Such composers as Mozart and Beethoven wrote music for it.
Glee. Eighteenth century English choral music, unaccompanied, in three or more parts. Entertainment music.
Gleichmässig (G, glykh'mays-sig). Even.

Glissando-Great Organ

Glissando (It, glee-sahn'doh). Slurred, smooth, in a gliding manner. Sliding the finger.

Glocke (G, glock'keh). Bell.

Glockenspiel (G, glock'n-shpeel). Percussion instrument made of a series of steel plates arranged like the piano keyboard. The plates are struck with wooden hammers.

Gondellied (G, gahn'dehl-leed), **gondoliera** (It, gahn-doh-lee-ehr'ah). Boat song.

Gong. Percussion instrument of Asian origin made of a circular piece of metal with a rim several inches deep. It is struck either by a wooden mallet covered with leather or felt, or by a stick similar to that used for the bass drum. Gongs with knobs are tunable; flat gongs such as the tam-tam are of indefinite pitch.

Grace. Ornament, embellishment.

Grace note. Ornamental note printed small to indicate that its time value is not counted in the rhythm of the measure and must be subtracted from that of an adjacent note. Large groups of grace notes are sometimes an exception to this rule and fill up the time value of a single note that has been omitted.

Gradatamente (It, grah-dah-tah-mehn'teh). By degrees, gradually.

Gradevole (It, grah-day'voh-leh). Pleasant, pleasing.

Gran (It, grahn). Large, great, full.

Grand', grande (F). Large, complete.

Grand jeu, grand orgue (F). Full organ.

Grand opera. Serious, fully composed text.

Grandezza (It, grahn-deht'sah). Grandeur, dignity.

Grand Positif. Great and choir organ coupled.

Grand Recitatif. Great and swell organ coupled.

Grave (It, grah'veh). Grave, solemn.

Gravicembalo (It, grah'vee-chem' bah-loh). Seventeenth century name for the harpsichord.

Grazia, grazioso (It). Grace, gracefully.

Great Organ. The principal manual of an organ located below the Swell Organ and above the Choir Organ. Its chief function is to provide massive sonority and brilliance even though it may also have a few soft stops.

Gross, grosse (G). Large, great.
Grosso (It). Great, grand, full, heavy.
Ground bass. A continually repeated bass pattern.
Guaracha (S). Cuban folksong.
Guarania (S). Paraguayan ballad in slow waltz tempo and usually in the minor mode.
Guasa (S). Satirical Venezuelan folk song.
Guida (It, gwee′dah). Subject of a fugue.
Guidon (F). A direct.
Guimbarde (F). Jew's harp.
Guitar. Plucked stringed instrument similar to the lute, but with a flat back and curved body similar to that of a violin. In 16th century Spain, several types of guitars were popular, those used for artistic works and those for popular folk music. In the 17th century, the guitar rose to prominence in other countries as an instrument easier to play than the lute. It has become a popular instrument in the late 20th century for folk, pop, and concert music.
Guitar family. Instruments with the general characteristics of the lute family, but that have the flat body of the guitar. Some instruments of the guitar family include: guitar, cittern, chitarra, battente, balalaika, ukulele, banjo, bandurria, and yueqin.
Gusle (Slav, goos′leh). Balkan one-stringed instrument played with a bow. It is used to accompany the chanting of Slavic epic poems.
Gusto, con (It, goo′stoh). With style, taste.

H

H. (1) In Germany, B natural. (2) Abbr. for Horn in orchestral scores; for Hand in piano music.

Habanera (S). Cuban dance.

Halb (G, hahlp). Half.

Half-step. The smallest interval in the musical system of twelve tones to the octave.

Hammerklavier (G, hah′mer-klah-veer′). Early 19th century name for the piano.

Hand organ. Portable barrel organ.

Handtrommel (G). Tambourine.

Hardanger fiddle. Norwegian folk instrument shaped somewhat like a violin, but slightly smaller and with a flatter bridge. It has four melody strings plus four or five sympathic strings.

Harfe (G, hahr′feh). Harp.

Harmonia (Greek). 'Fitting together'. Well-ordered, in harmony.

Harmonic. One of a series of tones that sounds with the fundamental tone when an elastic body is set in vibration.

Harmonica. Mouth organ. Popular instrument made of a small, flat metal box with slitlike openings on one of its horizontal sides. Inside each slit is a pair of reeds, one of which works by pressure and the other by suction. The player places the harmonica against his lips and blows or inhales to produce the desired tones.

Harmonic analysis. Study of individual chords or harmonies and their successive use in a piece of music.

Harmonic mark. The sign [○] placed over notes to be touched, not stopped, on stringed instruments.

Harmonic minor scale. See page 11.

Harmonic rhythm. Rhythmic pattern that is the result of the changes in harmony.

Harmonics-Heftig

Harmonics. Harmonics of a violin are high tones of a flutelike timbre produced by lightly touching the string at one of its nodes (fractional points) instead of pressing it down as in normal stopping. Touching a string lightly at its halfway point will produce a harmonic an octave higher than the open string.

Harmonic series. The series of acoustical harmonies or overtones.

Harmonium. A popular portable organ, activated by 2 pedals with both feet operating one after another to pump air. It used to be very popular at home and in small churches as a substitute for the pipe organ.

Harmony. The agreement of two or more united sounds. The art of combining sounds into chords.

Harp. Stringed instrument of ancient origin. The modern harp has a range of six octaves plus five degrees with seven strings to the octave. Seven pedals alter the pitch of the strings so that all Keys may be played.

Harp lute. An early 19th century instrument that combined features of the guitar and harp.

Harpsichord. Keyboard instrument that usually resembles the shape of a grand piano. The strings are plucked by a quill or leather tongue attached to a jack. Most harpsichords have two keyboards, but some smaller ones have only one. The harpsichord became popular in the 17th century generally replacing the lute. In the 18th century, it was used for solos, ensemble, and for accompanying singing. Its use was revived in the 20th century.

Hastig (G). With haste, hurrying.

Hatzotzcrah. Biblical trumpet.

Haupt (G). Head, principal.

Hauptwerk (G howpt'vehrk). Great Organ.

Hausmusik (G). Music for home use, in contrast to music for public performance.

Haut, haute (F, oh, oht). High.

Hautbois (F, oh-bwah'), **hautboy** (Engl. hoh-boy). Oboe.

Head. (1) Membrane stretched over a drum, tambourine, or banjo. (2) Point of a bow. (3) Scroll and peg box of a violin.

Headvoice. Higher register of a voice.

Heftig (G). Violent, vehement.

Heiter-Hornpipe

Heiter (G, hy-ter). Cheerful, glad.
Heldentenor (G). Tenor voice of great brilliance and volume suited for operatic parts.
Helicon. Brass instrument. (1) Bass and contrabass tuba in a circular shape so that a player may carry it on his shoulder. (2) An American sousaphone.
Hemidemisemiquaver. Sixty-fourth note.
Hemiola, hemiolia (G). Ratio of 3:2. In pitch, hemiola means the fifth, since the lengths of two strings sounding this interval are in the ratio 3:2. Also refers to time values that are in this ratio.
Hemitonium. Half-step.
Hervorgehoben (G, hair-fohr'geh-hoh'bn). Emphasized, prominent.
Hes (G, hehs). B flat.
Heses (G, hehs'ess). B double flat.
Hexachord. First six tones of a major scale; used in medieval theory.
Hichiriki. A Japanese oboe.
Hidden fifth, octaves. Parallel fifths, octaves.
Hilfslinie (G, hihlfs'lee'nee-eh). Leger line.
Hinsterbend (G, hin-shtair-behnt). Fading away.
Hirtenflöte (G, heer'tehn-fluh'tuh). Shepherd's pipe.
His (G, hiss). B sharp.
Hold. Same as pause.
Holz- (G, hohlts). Prefix meaning 'wood'.
Homo-, iso-. Prefixes meaning 'same' or 'equal'.
Homophonic. Alike in sound or pitch.
Homophony. Music in which one voice leads melodically and is supported by an accompaniment in chordal or more elaborate style. Nearly all music of the 19th century is homophonic.
Homorhythmic. Music that is polyphonic in which the voices move in the same rhythm producing a succession of chords, e.g. hymns and chorale melodies.
Horn. Brass instrument.
Hornpipe. (1) Old wind instrument. (2) Old dance usually in triple time.

Hummel-Hypo-

Hummel (G). Swedish zither with frets. Also, formerly, drone of bagpipes.

Humoreske (G), **humoresque** (F). Instrumental composition of the 19th century of a humorous or fanciful nature.

Hurdy-gurdy. Medieval stringed instrument shaped somewhat like a lute, whose strings are put in vibration by a rotating, rosined wheel operated by a handle. Two of the strings are affected by certain keys while the others serve as a drone bass.

Hurtig (G, hoor'tikh). Quick, nimble.

Hydraulos. Organ of ancient Greece whose wind supply was provided by water.

Hymn. Song of praise and adoration to God. In ancient times, a song in honor of gods or heroes.

Hyper- (Greek). Prefix meaning above, over.

Hypo- (Greek). Prefix meaning below, under.

I

I. (It, ee). Masculine plural article 'the'.
Iconography of music. The representation of musical instruments, musicians, and the like in sculpture, painting, mosaics, coins, etc. An important source of information.
Ictus. Stress or accent.
Idiomatic style. Refers to the writing of music that is appropriate for the instrument.
Idyl, idyll. Composition of pastoral or romantic character.
Imbroglio (It, eem-broh'lee-oh). Operatic scene in which the idea of utter confusion is carried out by giving the singers parts that are coordinated harmonically, but are deliberately contrasting in rhythm. The three orchestras in the ballroom scene of Mozart's *Don Giovanni* and the street scene from Wagner's *Die Meistersinger* are examples.
Imitation. In a contrapuntal work, the restatement of a theme or motif in different parts successively.
Imitative counterpoint. (1) Use of the same thematic material in all parts. (2) Canon, fugue, motet.
Impresario. Agent or manager of musical performers.
Impressionism. A period of artistic development of the late 19th and early 20th centuries represented in music chiefly by Claude Debussy (1862–1918). The term is borrowed from painting. Prominent are unresolved dissonances, mostly triads with added seconds, fourths, sixths, sevenths; the use of chords in parallel motion; the whole-tone scale; use of tritone; modality; avoidance of leading tone; avoidance of direction in melodic contour; and irregular and fragmentary construction of phrases.
Impromptu. Nineteenth century character piece.

Improvisation-Instruments

Improvisation. The art of performing music ectemporaneously. Also, the art of introducing improvised details into written compositions.

Incidental music. Music written as a supplement to a spoken play.

Inégales. Abbr. for *notes inégales* (F, nawts an-ay-gahl′). Performance of evenly written notes unequally with alternation between longer and shorter values.

Inflection. Any change or modification in the pitch or tone of the voice.

Innig (G). Heartfelt, tender, sincere.

Inno (It, een-noh). Hymn.

Instrumental music. Music performed on instruments as opposed to vocal music.

Instrumentation. The art of composing, arranging, or adapting music for a body of instruments of different kinds, especially for orchestra.

Instruments. Name for all devices that produce musical sounds. Instruments may be classified in four categories: (1) stringed instruments, usually called *chordophones* (Gr, *chordos,* strings; *phonos,* sound); (2) *aerophones* (Gr, *aeros,* air, wind); (3) percussion, which are divided into two classes: *idiophones* (Gr, *idios,* self), instruments that are self vibrating, and *membranophones* (Lat, *membranum,* skin), instruments for which a stretched skin is the sound producing agent; (4) *electrophones,* in which the acoustical vibrations are produced by electrical devices.

Instruments Classified
1. Stringed - Chordophones
   A. Percussion
      Piano
      Dulcimer
      Cimbalon
      Pantaleon

Instruments-Instruments

    B. Bowed
        Violin
        Viola
        Violoncello
        Double bass
        Viol
        Vielle
        Hurdy-gurdy
    C. Plucked
        Lute
        Harpsichord
        Guitar
        Zither
        Harp
        Banjo
        Psaltery
    D. Tangent
        Clavichord

2. Wind - Aerophones
    A. Enclosed Column Of Air
        Woodwind
        Flute
        Clarinet
        Bass Clarinet
        Oboe
        English Horn
        Bassoon
        Contrabassoon
    B. Brass
        Cornet
        Trumpet
        French Horn
        Trombone
        Tuba
        Saxhorn
        Bugle
        Saxophone
        Sousaphone
    C. Free Reeds
        Harmonium

Accordion
Regal
Sheng
Reed section of the Organ
3. **Percussion**
   A. Idiophones
      Triangle
      Gong
      Bells
      Chimes
      Glockenspiel
      Cymbals
      Xylophone
      Celesta
      Castanets
      Gambang
   B. Membranophones
      Drum
      Kettledrum
      Bass Drum
      Kazoo
4. **Electrophones, electronic instruments**
   A. Amplified
      Stringed Instruments, Violin Family
      Guitar
      Piano
      Carillon
   B. Generated
      Electronic Organ
      Synthesizer

Interlude. Any kind of inserted music.
Intermezzo (It, in-ter-meht′tsoh). Light, entertainment music.
Interpretation. The personal and creative element in the performance of music. In addition to personal taste, historical fact enters into interpretation.
Interval. The distance in pitch between two tones. The interval is counted from the lower tone to the higher tone. See chart of Intervals on pages 7–8.
Intonation. (1) Singing or playing in tune. (2) The opening notes of a chant.

Intrada-Istesso

Intrada (It, in-trah′dah). Short prelude or introduction.
Intrepido (It, een-tray′pee-doh). Bold, intrepid.
Introduction. A phrase or section preceding a composition.
Invention. Short piece in free contrapuntal style.
Inversion. Change of position of notes of intervals and chords, the lower notes placed above and vice versa. *Harmonic inversion:* an interval or chord is inverted by transferring its lower note into the higher octave. *Melodic inversion:* changing each ascending interval into the corresponding descending interval and vice versa.
Inverted canon. Changed by melodic inversion or retrograde motion.
Inverted fugue. Counterfugue.
Ionian. See Modes.
Isometric (eye-suh-meh′trik). Term used for polyphonic music in which all the parts move at the same time in the same rhythmic values, forming a succession of chords.
Istesso (It, ees-stehs′soh). Same. *Istesso tempo,* indication that the duration of the beat remains unaltered even though the meter changes.

J

Jack. An upright slip of wood on the rear end of the key lever carrying a piece of quill to pluck the string of a harpsichord.
Jagd- (G, yahkht-). Hunt.
Jagdhorn (G). Hunting horn.
Jagdstück, Jagdmusik (G). Hunting piece.
Jam. Jazz musician's name for improvisation. At a jam session, several musicians improvise on a familiar tune.
Janko keyboard. A piano keyboard invented by Paul von Janko of Hungary in 1882. It has six rows of keys so arranged that any given tone can be played in three different places.
Jazz. General term for wide variety of 20th century styles of principally African American origin. It was first identified with social dancing and featured patterns peculiar to the "jazz beat." Most jazz incorporates improvisation as a centrtal element. Composers such as Copland and Milhaud have incorporated jazz elements into their concert works.
Jeu (F). Organ stop.
Jew's harp. A small instrument of brass or steel shaped like a horseshoe with a thin, vibrating tongue of metal. The frame is held between the teeth, and the elastic strip is plucked with the fingers.
Jig. English country dance in triple time.
Jodel, jodelyn, jodler. See Yodel.
Just intonation. System of tuning in which all the intervals are derived from the pure fifth and the pure third in contrast to tempered tuning.

K

K. With a number following, refers to the catalogue of Mozart's works complied by Ludwig von Köchel.
Kadenz. Cadence, cadenza.
Kammer (G). Chamber.
Kanon (G). Canon.
Kantate (G). Cantata.
Kanzone (G). Canzona.
Kapelle (G). Chapel. Small private orchestra or band.
Kapellmeister (G, kah-pehl-my-stehr). 'Master of the chapel', director of music to a prince, king, or other royalty.
Kapodaster (G). Capotasto.
Kazoo. Mirliton.
Kent bugle. A bugle with six keys.
Kesselpauke, Kesseltrommel (G). Kettledrum.
Kettledrum. Orchestral drum made of a hollow brass or copper kettle resting on a tripod, with a head of calf-skin stretched by means of an iron ring and tightened by a set of screws which change the pitch. They are generally played in pairs with one drum tuned to a higher pitch than the other.
Key. (1) Tonality, the main note of a composition, which is called the keynote. (2) The visible part of the action of a keyboard instrument. (3) Levers covering the side holes in woodwind instruments.
Keyboard. The rows of keys of piano, organs, harpsichords, and similar instruments.
Key characteristics. Branch of musical aesthetics concerned with the 'psychological properties' of a given Key or scale.
Keynote. The Tonic, or first note of a scale.
Key relationship. The degree of relationship between two keys.
Key signature. The sharps or flats placed at the beginning of the staff to indicate the Key of the composition. See pages 5–6.

Khorovod. Russian game dances and songs sung in chorus in two or more parts.
Kin. Japanese name for the Chinese qin.
Kirche (G, keer'shuh). Church.
Kit. A "pocket-sized" violin about 16 inches long used by dancing-masters of the 17th and 18th century.
Kithara. The foremost instrument of ancient Greece. It consisted of a square wooden soundbox and two curved arms connected by a crossbar. It had from 5 to 11 strings, plucked with a plectrum.
Klagend (G, klah'gehnt). Lamenting.
Klang (G). Sound, sonority.
Klangfarbe (G, klahng'fahr-buh). Tone color.
Klappe (G). Key of wind instruments.
Klar (G). Clear, distinct.
Klarinette (G). Clarinet.
Klaviatur (G). Keyboard.
Klavier (G, klah-veer). Clavier.
Knarre (G, k-nahr'ruh). Ratchet.
Kniegeige (G, k-nee'guy-guh). Viola da gamba.
Konzert (G). Concert, concerto.
Koppel (G). Coupler.
Koto. Japanese stringed instrument.
Kräftig (G, krehf-tigh). Strong, forceful.
Kreuz (G, kroytz). Sharp.
Kurz (G, koorts). Short.

L

L. Abbr. for Left. (*L. H.,* left hand).
La. Sixth syllable of the Major scale.
Labial pipes. Flue stops.
Lacrimoso (It, lah-kree-moh'zoh). Mournful.
Lage (G, lah'guh). Position of a chord or of the hand.
Lagnoso (It, lahn-yoh'zoh). Lamenting.
Lamento (It). Music of a mournful character.
Lancio, con (It, kohn lahn'choh). With vigor.
Landler (G, lehnt'lair). Austrian dance much like a slow waltz.
Langsam (G, lahng'zahm). Slow.
Largamente (It, lahr-gah-mehn'teh). Broadly.
Largando (It, lahr-gahn'doh). Slowing down.
Larghetto (It, lahr-geht'toh). Not quite so slow as Largo.
Largo (It, lahr'goh). Very slow, usually with much expression.
Larigot (F, lah-ree-goh'). Shepherd's pipe. Organ stop.
Lauda (It, from Latin, loud'ah). Hymns of praise and devotion in the Italian language.
Lauf (G, louf). A rapid passage.
Laute (G, lou'tuh). Lute.
Lay. A melody or tune.
Leader. Conductor, in America; concertmaster, in England.
Leading tone. The seventh degree of the scale, one-half step below the Tonic.
Lebendig (G, lay'behn'digh). Lively.
Ledger lines. Leger lines.
Legatissimo (It, leh-gah-tees'see-moh). Very smooth and connected.
Legato (It, leh-gah'toh). Bound, slurred. In a smooth, connected manner.
Legend, legende. A piece written in a romantic, narrative style.
Leger lines. Additional lines added above or below the staff for notes that are too high or too low to be written on the staff.

Leggero (It, leh-jay'roh), **leggiero** (It, leh-jee-ehr'oh). Light, airy, swift, delicate.
Legno (It, leh'nyoh). Wood.
Legno, col (It). In violin playing, tapping the strings with the stick of the bow instead of bowing.
Leidenshaftlich (G). Passionately.
Leier (G). The lyre. In earlier usage, the hurdy-gurdy.
Leierkasten (G). Street organ.
Leise (G, lye-zuh). Low, soft.
Leiter (G, lye-tair). (1) Scale. (2) Orchestra leader.
Leitmotiv (G, lye-t-moh-teef'). Well marked theme or motif.
Leitton (G, lye-ton). Leading tone.
Lento (It, lehn'toh). Slow, slowly.
Libretto (It, lee-breht'toh). Text of an opera, oratorio, etc.
Licenza (It, lee-chehn'tsah). Freedom, leeway, flexibility in execution.
Lied (G, leet). Song.
Liedform (G). Song form.
Lieto (It, lee-eh'toh). Gay, joyful.
Lievo (It, lee-eh'voh). Light, easy.
Ligature. (1) Old name for Tie. (2) A group of notes executed in one breath or phrase.
Linear counterpoint. Twentieth century way of composing counterpoint that gives priority to the horizontal lines of each part individually. Sometimes the result is harmonic dissonance. An effective sound is created when each part is given to an instrument of a different tone color in contrast to all string instruments, for example.
Linke Hand (G, lin'keh hahnt). Left hand.
Lip. Embouchure.
Lira (It, lee'rah). Fifteenth and 16th century type of violin in two sizes: the *lira da braccio* played on the arm and the *lira da gamba* played between the knees. Both had drone strings.
Liscio (It, lee'shoh). Smooth, flowing.
L'istesso (It, lee-steh'soh). The same.
Liuto (It, lew'toh). Lute.
Livret (F, lee-vreh'). Libretto.
Loco (It, from Latin). Place; following 8va, it means 'perform the notes as written'.
Locrian. See Modes.

Lontano-Lyric

Lontano (It, lohn-tah'noh). Far away, as from a distance.
Lourd (F, loor), **lourde** (F, loord). Heavy.
Louré (F, loo-ray'). Slurred, legato.
Luftpause (G, looft'pow-zuh). Breathing rest.
Lusingando (It, loo-zeen-gahn'doh). Caressing.
Lustig (G, loos'tigh). Merry, cheerful, gay.
Lute. Plucked stringed instrument with half-pear shaped body and fretted fingerboard. A separate pegbox is set perpendicular to the neck.
Lute harpsichord. A harpsichord that has strings of gut instead of metal.
Luttuoso (It, loo-too-oh'soh). Mournful, sad.
Lydian. See Modes.
Lyra, lyre. Ancient Greek stringed instrument with a soundbox often made of tortoiseshell. The strings, plucked with a plectrum, were attached to a crossbar that joined the two curving arms.
Lyra piano. Early 19th century upright piano with a case shaped like a lyre.
Lyric. Song-like, appropriate for singing.

M

M. Abbr. for Mezzo, Manual, Metronome, Main, and Mano.

Madrigal. Vocal composition in three to six parts originally from Italy, further developed in England during the 16th century.

Maestoso (It, mah-ehs-toh'so). Majestic.

Maestro (It, mah-yes'troh). Honorary title for distinguished teachers, composers, or conductors.

Magadis. Ancient Greek harp with ten pairs of strings, each pair tuned to the fundamental and its octave. The term 'magadizing' is sometimes used to describe singing in octaves.

Maggiore (It, mah-jor'reh). Major Key.

Main (F). Hand.

Majeur (F, mah-zhoor'). Major.

Major. With respect to intervals, greater. A Key is called Major when it is based on the Major scale.

Major scale. Diatonic scale in which the half-steps occur between the 3rd and 4th degrees and the 7th and 8th degrees.

Malagueña (S, mah-lah-gwayn'yah). A type of Spanish folk music.

Malincolico, malinconico (It). In a melancholy style.

Man. Abbr. for Manual.

Manche (F, mahnsh). Neck of the violin.

Mandola, mandora (It). Type of lute.

Mandolin. The most recent instrument of the lute family. In general use in southern Italy. It has eight wire strings in pairs tuned like the violin and played with a plectrum.

Manica (It). In violin playing, a shift of hand position.

Manico (It). Fingerboard of the violin.

Manicordion, manichord. Sixteenth century name for Clavichord.

Manieren (G). Eighteenth century name for ornaments of a restricted melodic range.

Mannheim School. Important group of composers of the mid 18th century centered in Mannheim, Germany.
Mano destra (It, mah-noh deh′strah). Abbr. M.d. Right hand.
Mano sinistra (It, mah-noh see-nee′strah). Abbr. M.s. Left hand.
Manual. Organ keyboards for the hands as opposed to the *pedalboard* for the feet. The keyboards of the harpsichord are also called manuals.
Manualiter. In organ playing, on the manuals alone.
Manualkoppel (G). Manual coupler.
Manubrio (It). Knobs and handles of organ stops.
Maraca. Latin American rhythm instrument made of a gourd containing dry seeds. Shaken by a handle, it is often played in pairs.
Marcando, marcato (It). Marked, stressed.
March. Piece of music with a strongly marked rhythm suitable for marching.
Marcia, alla (It, ahl′lah mahr′chee-ah). In the manner of a march.
Mariachi (S). Mexican ensemble of a variable number of musicians.
Marimba. Type of xylophone made of wooden bars suspended in a frame with a resonator under each bar. Played with rubber or felt-headed mallets.
Markiert (G). Marked, stressed.
Markig (G). Vigorous.
Marqué (F, mahr-kay'). Marked, stressed.
Marsch (G). March.
Martelé (F, mahr-teh-lay′), **martelatto** (It, mahr-teh-lah′toh). 'Hammering'. On the violin, playing the notes with a sharp, decided stroke. On the piano, a forceful, detached touch.
Masculine, feminine cadence. Cadence is referred to as 'masculine' when the final chord occurs on the strong beat, as 'feminine' when it falls on a weak beat.
Masque, mask. A musical drama of the 16th and 17th centuries that combined poetry, vocal and instrumental music, dancing, and acting.
Mazurka. Polish folk dance in triple meter.
M.d. Abbr. for *Main droite* (F), or *Mano destra* (It). Right hand.
Me. *Mi* in Tonic Sol-fa.

Meane-Mesure

Meane, mene. In 15th to 17th century English music, the middle part of a polyphonic composition.
Measure. The metrical unit in music with regular accents. The notes and rests between two bar lines on the staff.
Mechanical instruments. Devices designed to produce music mechanically without the aid of a performer.
Medesimo (It, meh-day'zee-moh). Same.
Mediant. The third degree of a scale.
Medley. Series of popular tunes, operatic airs, patriotic songs or the like, played in succession and connected by a few measures of introduction or modulation.
Mehr (G). More, several.
Meistersinger (G). A member of one of the song schools of the 15th and 16th century craft-guilds that developed the tradition of the Minnesinger into a musical and literary movement.
Mejorana (S). Song of Spanish origin brought to Panama during the 18th century.
Mejoranera (S). Five-stringed guitar of Panama.
Melisma. Expressive vocal passage sung to one syllable.
Melodica. A wind instrument with a small keyboard. The tone is much like that of a recorder. Chords can be sounded by playing more than one key at a time.
Melodrama. Stage presentation in which background music accompanies spoken parts.
Melody. A succession of musical tones.
Membranophone. An instrument in which a stretched skin or parchment is the sound-producing agent.
Même (F). Same.
Meno (It, may'noh). Less.
Mensur (G). Meter, mensuration.
Mensural music. Polyphonic music in which each note has a strictly determined value.
Mente, alla (It). Improvised.
Menuet (F), **menuett** (G). Minuet.
Messa di voce (It, mehs'sah dee voh'cheh). Special 18th century vocal technic consisting of a gradual crescendo and decrescendo over a sustained tone.
Mesto (It). Sad, mournful, melancholy.
Mesure (F). Measure or meter.

Meter-Misterioso

Meter, metre. The pattern of regularly recurring accents indicated by the time signature. The groupings are indicated by bar lines that mark off the measure.

Metric notation. Rhythm notation that matches horizontal space to duration, i.e. a half note has twice the space of a quarter note.

Metronome. A device that ticks regular beats at adjustable speeds. It indicates the tempo of a composition and gives a steady speed. Electrical and battery operated metronomes are available as well as the pendulum swinging model.

Metronomic marks. On a piece of music, the numbers corresponding to those on a metronome to indicate tempo, i.e. 96 quarter notes per minute. [♩ = 96]

Mezzo, mezza (It, mehh′tsoh, met′sah). Half.

Mezzo forte (It). Abbr. [*mf*] Half loud, moderately loud.

Mezzo piano (It). Abbr. [*mp*] half soft, moderately soft.

Mezzo soprano. The female voice between soprano and alto.

Mezzo voce (It, meht′tsoh voh′cheh). Half voice.

Mi. The third syllable or degree of a scale.

Microtone. An interval smaller than a half-step.

Middle C. The C in the middle of the piano keyboard.

Mineur (F). Minor.

Minim. British name for half note.

Minim rest. Half rest.

Minnesinger (G). German troubadour of the 12th and 13th centuries.

Minor. Lesser, smaller.

Minstrel. Originally, the professional musician of the Middle Ages. Modern usage covers a large area of entertainment music.

Minuet. French country dance in 3/4 time that became a dance of the French courts.

Mirliton. A membrane that when added to an instrument modifies its sound. Instruments incorporating a mirliton include the kazoo and the Chinese dizi.

Mirror composition. Composition in retrograde or inverted intervals.

Misterioso (It, mee-steh-ree-oh′soh). In a mysterious manner, mysteriously.

Misura (It, mee-zoo′rah). Measure, beat.
Mit (G). With.
Mixolydian. See Modes.
M.M. Maelzel's Metronome.
Mobile (It, moh′bee-leh). Changeable, movable.
Modal. Pertaining to a Mode.
Modality. The use of modes other than major and minor modes (tonality). The term refers to modal idioms of the 19th and 20th centuries.
Modal rhythm. Rhythm based on the rhythmic modes.
Mode. Term used for two entirely different ideas, both taken from medieval music: (1) scale formation; (2) rhythm. (1) In the broadest sense of the word, mode means the selection of tones, a scale, that makes up the tonality of a composition. See pages 11–12.
Moderato (It, moh-day-rah′toh). Moderately, in moderate time.
Moderno (It, moh-dair′noh). Modern, in modern style.
Modes, rhythmic. Thirteenth century system of rhythm in which simple rhythm patterns are repeated.
Modulate. To pass from one Key to another.
Modulation. Change of Key within a composition.
Moll (g). Minor Key.
Molto (It, mohl′toh). Much, very.
Monacordo (It). Sixteenth century name for clavichord.
Monochord. Instrument consisting of one string stretched over a wooden resonator. It is used to demonstrate the relation between musical intervals and the division of the string.
Monody. Solo song with accompaniment.
Monophony, monophonic. Music with a single melody line without additional parts or accompaniment.
Monotone. Single, unaccompanied, and unvaried tone.
Morceau (F, mohr-soh′). Piece, composition.
Mordent. An ornament consisting of an alternation of the written note with the note immediately below it.
Morendo (It). Fading away.
Mosso (It). Moved, agitated.
Motet. Unaccompanied choral composition.
Motif, motive. Short phrase or figure used throughout a composition or section as a unifying element.

Motion-Muta

Motion. Pattern of changing pitch levels, high and low, in a melody. Also, the changes of pitch in two or more voice parts.

Moto (It). Motion.

Mouth organ. Harmonica.

Mouthpiece. The part of a wind instrument that a player places upon or between his lips.

Mouvement (F, moov-mahn'). Movement, tempo.

Movable Do. Syllabic system so designed that the syllables can be transposed into any Key in contrast to the 'Fixed Do' in which the syllables correspond to specific pitches.

Movement. Principal division or section of a composition.

Multimetric. Metric pattern in which the meter changes frequently, e.g., two measures of $\frac{3}{4}$ followed by one measure $\frac{2}{4}$. It is common in the works of 20th century composers.

Mundharmonika (G). Mouth organ.

Munter (G, moon'ter). Merry, cheerful.

Murky. Bass accompaniment in broken octaves. It was used in the 18th century.

Musette, musetta. (1) French bagpipe of the 17th and 18th centuries. (2) Dance pieces with a long-held drone.

Music. The term is derived from the Greek word 'muse' and more specifically the Art of the Muses. (1) The art and science of combining vocal or instrumental sounds in varying melody, harmony, rhythm, and timbre so as to form structurally complete and emotionally expressive compositions. (2) Any rhythmic sequence of pleasing sounds, as of birds, water, etc. (3) The written or printed score of a piece of music.

Musica (L). Music.

Music box. A mechanical device with a metal cylinder, or barrel, studded with pins and turned by clockwork. In turning, the pins catch and twang a comb-like row of steel teeth, each tooth producing a tone.

Musical saw. A handsaw held between the knees and set in vibration by either a violin bow or drumstick.

Musicology. The scholarly study of music.

Music therapy. The use of music in medical treatment.

Muta (It, moo'tah). 'Change'. Indication for a change of tuning in the orchestral parts for kettledrums.

Mutation-Mute

Mutation. (1) Change of voice. (2) In violin playing, a shift of position.

Mute. Device for softening or muffling the tone of a musical instrument. On violins the mute is a clamp fitted to the bridge. Brass instruments are muted by inserting a pear-shaped piece of wood or metal into the bell. The French horn is usually muted by the player's hand. In pianos, the sound is muted by the left pedal that causes the whole keyboard with the hammers to shift sideways so that the hammers strike one string instead of three strings.

N

Nachamung (G, nakh-ahm′oong). Imitation.
Nachdrücklich (G). Emphatic, expressive.
Nachlassend (G). Relaxing, slackening.
Nachschlag (G). The end note of a trill.
Nachspiel (G, nakh-shpeel). Postlude.
Nachtmusik (G). Night music, serenade.
Nachtstück (G). Nocturne.
Naked fifth. Open fifth.
Narrator. In oratorios, cantatas, operas, etc., the character who tells the basic story, usually in recitative.
Natural. (1) A note that is neither flat nor sharp. (2) The sign [♮].
Natural horn. Horn or trumpet consisting of just a pipe, no keys or valves.
Neck. The part of a violin, lute, guitar, etc., by which the instrument is held.
Neoclassicism. Movement of the 20th century in which composers have included features of 17th and 18th century music. It is a reaction against Romanticism and program music; a revival of many early forms and styles.
Neomodal. Refers to the use of modal idioms in contemporary music.
Neue Musik (G). Twentieth century music.
Neumes. Notational signs of the Middle Ages that were used for writing down plainsong.
Nineteenth. Interval of two octaves and a fifth.
Ninth. Interval of an octave plus a major or minor second.
Ninth chord. Third, fifth, seventh, and ninth above the root.
Nobilemente (It, non-beel-eh-men′teh). Grand, lofty, impressive, noble.
Nocturne. A composition of dreamy, romantic character.

Nodes. (1) The points of rest or of minimum amplitude in a vibrating string. Such points occur at the two fixed ends of a string and also at regular points in between, due to the fact that the string vibrates not only as a whole, but also in segments — $1/2$, $1/3$, $1/4$, $1/5$, etc., of its length. Harmonics on a violin are produced by touching the string at one of these nodes. (2) Nodes are the highest density in a vibrating air column (pipe), where the air particles do not move. The intermediate points of maximum amplitude (string), or movement (pipe) are called loops or antinodes.

Noel (F). Christmas carol or hymn.

Non (It, nohn). Not, no.

Nonet. Composition for nine instruments.

Nonharmonic tones. Tones that are foreign to the harmony of the moment and occur as melodic ornamentations in one of the parts.

Notation. Methods used for writing down music.

Notes. Signs with which music is written on the staff. See page 3.

Notturno, nocturne. Eighteenth century names for compositions similar to the serenade, designed to be played as evening entertainment.

Nourri, bien (F). With richness of sound.

Nowell. Old English spelling of *Noel*.

Nuances (F). Shading; subtle changes of intensity, tempo, touch, and phrasing.

Nut. Small bridge at the upper end of the fingerboard of a guitar or violin over which the strings pass to the pegs.

O

O. Sign used (1) by the medieval monks to indicate triple time; (2) for open strings; (3) in thorough-bass parts for tasto solo; (4) for diminished.
Obbligato (It). Required, obligatory. An obbligato part is essential.
Ober (G). Upper, higher.
Oberdominante (G). Dominant in contrast to Unterdominante, subdominant.
Oberstimme (G). Upper part.
Obertaste (G). Black key of the piano.
Oberton, obertöne (G). Upper harmonic(s).
Oberwerk (G). Swell Organ.
Obligat (G). Obbligato.
Oblique motion. When one part ascends or descends while the other part remains the same pitch.
Oboe. Wind instrument dating from the 17th century made of a conical pipe with a double reed fixed to the upper end. It has a penetrating nasal tone quality which makes it an effective solo instrument in the orchestra.
Ocarina. Perhaps from Italian 'oca' (goose) which its shape resembles, the 'sweet potato' is a keyless terra cotta or plastic instrument properly classified as a globular flute.
Octave. (1) The series of eight diatonic degrees; (2) the interval spanned by two tones, the higher of which has twice the frequency of the lower.
Octave marks. Abbr. 8va or 8 followed by a dotted line means that the notes over which it is placed are to be played an octave higher than written until the end of the dotted line or the word *loco*. When an octave lower is to be played, the sign and dotted line are placed below the notes.
Octet. Composition for eight parts.
Oeuvre (F). Opus.

Oktave - Orchestration

Oktave (G). Octave. Applied to instruments the sizes an octave above the normal size.

Oliphant. Medieval horn for signaling, made from an elephant's tusk or of gold.

Ondeggiando (It), **ondulé** (F). In violin playing, an undulating movement of the bow.

Onzième (F). Interval of the eleventh.

Open fifth, open triad. Fifth or triad without the third.

Open notes. On wind instruments, the natural notes; on stringed instruments, open strings.

Open strings. The unstopped strings of violins, lutes, etc. Shown by the sign 0.

Opera. A drama in which the essential factor is music comprising sung text with orchestral accompaniment and orchestral preludes and interludes.

Opéra bouffe (F), **opera buffa** (It). Comic opera, often satirical.

Opéra comique (F). Comic opera.

Opera seria (It). Serious opera. Grand, heroic, tragic.

Operetta. Light opera, usually short.

Ophicleide. Old brass instrument of the key-bugle family; forerunner of the tuba.

Opus (L). (1) Work. (2) Number generally used to indicate the order in which works were composed.

Oratorio. Setting of a text on a sacred or epic theme for chorus, soloists, and orchestra for performance in a church or concert hall.

Orchestra. Large ensemble of instruments in contrast to small ensembles used for chamber music. The symphony orchestra has from about 60 to 100 players.

Orchestration. The art of writing music for performance by an orchestra; the science of combining in an effective manner the instruments of the orchestra.

Organ (pipe)-Overture

Organ (pipe). Keyboard instrument consisting of a series of pipes and a wind chest. The wind chest is fitted with valves connected to the keys, either by direct mechanical linkage or by electrical and/or pneumatic means. The simplest organ has one set of pipes, each pipe corresponding to one key of the keyboard. Organs usually have several sets, or 'ranks', of pipes to make available a variety of tone colors. An organ usually has a minimum of two manuals and a pedalboard. Organs with three or four manuals are not unusual.

Organ chorale. Polyphonic composition for organ based on a chorale melody.

Organetto (It). Fourteenth century name for portative organ.

Organ point. Pedal point.

Orgel (G), **orgue** (F). Organ.

Ornamentation. The melodic figures that are substituted for or added to the original notes of the melody. Throughout music history there have been three kinds of ornaments: (1) left entirely to the improvisation of the performance; (2) definite ornaments indicated by written signs; (3) ornaments written out in notes.

Orphica. A variety of piano invented in 1795.

Ossia (It, ohs-see'ah). From 'or it may be', indicating an alternate version, title, etc.

Ostinato (It, oh-stee-nah'toh). Persistent, obstinate. A clearly defined theme that is repeated throughout a composition or section.

Ottava (It oht-tah'vah). Abbr. 8va or 8. Octave.

Ottava bassa (It). The octave below, marked 8va bassa.

Ottavino (It). the piccolo flute.

Ou (F, oo). Or; or else.

Ouverture. (F, oo-vair'tyoor'). Overture.

Overtone. Harmonic above the fundamental pitch.

Overture. A musical introduction to an opera, oratorio, or similar work.

P

P. Abbr. for Pedal (P. or Ped.); piano (*p*); in organ music, P means Positif or choir Organ.

Pacato (It, pah-kah′toh). Calm.

Padiglione. The bell of a wind instrument.

Pandoura, pandura. A long-necked lute of ancient Rome and Greece.

Panpipes. One of the oldest and simplest musical instruments. A set of graduated reeds or tubes arranged in a row and blown into by the mouth.

Pantomime. A silent dramatic performance in which the action is expressed by mimicry, facial expression, and gestures, sometimes accompanied by instrumental music.

Pantonality, pantonal. The inclusion of all tonalities.

Parallel chords. The movement of fixed chordal combinations through various degrees of the scale.

Parallel fifths, octaves. The duplication of the melodic progression of a part by another part at the interval of a fifth or octave.

Parallel intervals. Movement of two parts at the same time at the same interval.

Parallel Keys. Different Keys founded on the same Keynote.

Parallel motion. Two or more parts moving at the same distance apart in the same direction.

Paralleltonart (G). Relative Key.

Parameter. Mathematical term denoting special variables in acoustics. The term is used in 20th century music to indicate variabilities of pitch, volume, rhythm, timbre, etc.

Paraphrase. A transcription or arrangement of a composition with variations.

Parlando (It, pahr-lahn′doh). 'Speaking', in vocal music, an indication that the voice must approximate speech.

Parody. Satirical imitation.

Part-Pedalier

Part. (1) Music written for a particular instrument. (2) Single melodic line in counterpoint. (3) A section of a composition as in three-part form.

Partial. Harmonic.

Partimento (It). Seventeenth and 18th century practice of improvising melodies above written bass.

Partita (It, pahr-tee'tah). Variation.

Partition (F), **Partitur** (G), **partitura** (It). Score.

Part song. A melody harmonized by other parts. Counterpoint is usually not used.

Passacaglia. Old Italian dance in triple time usually written on a ground bass.

Passage. Short section of a composition.

Passaggio (It). Transition, modulation. Also passage work.

Passacaille (F). Passacaglia.

Passepied (F, pahs-pee-ay'). Gay French dance in quick $\frac{3}{8}$ or $\frac{6}{8}$ time.

Passing tones. Notes that do not belong to the chords, but pass from one chord to another.

Passionato (It, pah-see-oh-nah'toh). Fervently, passionately.

Pasticcio (It, pahs-tee'choh). A composition made up of works of more than one composer.

Pastoral. Instrumental piece written in imitation of the style and instruments of rural and idyllic scenes.

Patetico (It, pah-tay'tee-koh). With great emotion.

Pathetisch (G). With great emotion.

Patter song. Humorous song sung very fast.

Pauke (G). Kettledrum.

Pausa (It). Rest, a pause.

Pause. Rest, hold.

Pavane. Slow, processional type dance.

Peal. (1) Set of bells tuned to each other. (2) The changes rung upon a set of bells.

Pedal. An action operated by the feet.

Pedal harp. Modern chromatic harp.

Pedal harpsichord. Harpsichord that has a pedal board similar to that of the organ so that the bass can be played with the feet.

Pedalier (F, peh-dahl-yay'). Pedal board of an organ or a like apparatus attached to a piano.

Pedalklavier (G). Pedal piano.
Pedalkoppel (G). Pedal coupler of the organ.
Pedalpauke (G). Kettledrums tuned by pedals.
Pedal piano. Piano equipped with a pedal board like that of the organ so that the bass can be played with the feet.
Pedal point. A sustained note in the bass part sounding with changing harmonies in the other parts.
Peine entendu, à (F). Barely audible.
Pentachord. Five-tone segment of a scale.
Pentatonic scale. Scale of five tones to the octave, usually with the fourth and seventh tones of the major scale omitted.
Per (It). for, by, from, in, through.
Percussion. Instruments that are sounded by shaking or striking one object with another. See Instruments.
Perdendosi (It, pair-dehn′doh-see). Dying away.
Perfect. Term applied to certain intervals and cadences. See pages 7–8.
Perfect pitch. The faculty of a person to hear and identify a pitch by name without reference to another pitch.
Period. In traditional music, a musical sentence usually made up of two or more phrases and ending with a cadence.
Perpetuum mobile (Lat). Term used to describe pieces that proceed from beginning to end in the same rapid motion.
Pesante (It, peh-zahn′teh). Heavy, ponderous.
Petit (F, pih-tee′). Little, small.
Peu (F, pew). Little somewhat.
Pezzo (It, peht′soh). Composition, piece.
Pfeife (G). Fife; organ pipe.
Phantasie (G). Imaginative, fanciful pieces sometimes with a programmatic idea.
Phonetic. Vocal sounds.
Phonograph. Record player.
Phrase. A unit of the musical line somewhat comparable to a clause or sentence in prose.
Phrasing, articulation. Punctuation of music.
Phrygian. See Modes.
Piacere, a (It, ahp′yah-cheh′reh). 'At pleasure'. Expression is left to the performer.
Piacevole (It, p′yah-chay′voh-leh). Pleasing, agreeable.
Pianissimo (It). Abbr. [*pp*] Very soft.

Piano (It). Abbr. [*p*] Soft.

Piano, pianoforte. A stringed keyboard instrument of percussion. The tones are produced by hammers striking the strings. Since the end of the 18th century, it has been the main domestic keyboard instrument in Europe and America. Originally called the *pianoforte* (It, 'soft-loud'), in contrast to the earlier *harpsichord* whose volume could not be varied by the touch of the fingers as the piano can.

Piano duet. Composition for two pianists playing on either one or two instruments.

Piano, electronic. Twentieth century keyboard instrument whose tones are produced by reeds, strings, or other means, and amplified. It is used mainly in the entertainment field and by schools and universities in learning labs.

Piatti (It, pee-ah'tee). Cymbals.

Picardy third. Major third as used in the final chord of a composition in a minor Key.

Piccolo. Small flute.

Pick. Plectrum used to pluck the strings of a guitar, mandolin, etc.

Pieno (It, pee-eh'noh). Full.

Pince (F, pan'say). Lit. 'pinched'. (1) Plucked, as the strings of a harp. (2) Mordent. (3) In violin playing, pizzicato.

Pipa. Chinese pear-shaped lute with four strings.

Pipe. (1) Small instrument of the recorder type. (2) Wind instruments, the pipes of the organ, and primitive instruments in the shape of a tube.

Pistons. Mechanical devices on organs for making quick stop changes.

Pitch. Location of a musical sound in the tonal scale. Exact pitch is determined by the number of vibrations per second (frequency).

Pitch aggregate. A cluster of pitches.

Pitch pipe. A small reed pipe that sounds one or more tones of fixed pitch to give the tone for tuning an instrument or a choir.

Più (It, pew). More.

Piva. (1) Italian name for bagpipe. (2) Early 16th century fast dance.

Pivot chord. In modulation, a chord that is common to both the first Key and the new Key.
Pizzicato (It, pee-tsee-kah′toh). 'Pinched', or plucked with the finger. In music for bowed instruments, pluck the strings.
Placido (It, plah′chee-doh). Calm, tranquil.
Plagal cadence. Cadence with the Subdominant preceding the Tonic. IV-I.
Plainchant. Plainsong.
Plainsong. Ancient style of monophonic and rhythmically free melody, which is neither harmonic nor strictly measured.
Plainte (F, plehnt). Baroque ornament.
Plaisanterie (F, plehz-ahn-tree′). Lit. 'joking, spoofing'. (1) Collection of pieces in rococo style. (2) Light, gay movement found in 18th century music.
Plaqué (F). Indication for notes of a chord to be played together, not as an arpeggio.
Plectrum (Greek, 'pick'). Small quill or piece of ivory, wood, metal, or plastic, used to pluck the strings of certain stringed instruments.
Plein (F). Full.
Plein-jeu (F, plehn-zhoo′). Full organ.
Poco, un poco (It). Little; a little.
Poco a poco (It). Little by little.
Poi (It, poh-ee). Then, thereafter.
Point. Upper end of a violin bow.
Point d'orgue (F, pwan dorrg′). (1) Pedal point; (2) pause; (3) cadenza.
Polacca (It, poh-lahk′kah). Polonaise.
Polka. Bohemian dance in duple time.
Polonaise (F). Polish national dance of a stately, festive character in triple time. It usually has a persistent rhythm pattern and a feminine ending.
Poly-, multi-. Prefixes meaning 'many'.
Polychoral style. Composition in which the ensemble is divided into distinct groups performing singly, in alternation, and jointly.
Polymetric. Term used for vocal music in which the bar lines are placed at irregular intervals. This might better be called 'multimetric' with 'polymetric' reserved for the simultaneous use of different meters.

Polyphony-Prelude

Polyphony (pohl-if'oh-nee). Music that combines several voice parts of individual design at the same time.
Polyrhythm. The simultaneous use of contrasting rhythms.
Polytextuality. The simultaneous use of different texts in various parts of a composition.
Polytonality. The simultaneous use of two or more different Keys in different parts of a composition.
Pomposo (It, pohm-poh'soh). Pompous.
Ponticello (It, pohn-tee-cheh'loh). Bridge of stringed instruments.
Portamento (It). Smooth gliding from one note to another, differing from legato in its more deliberate execution and in the actual sounding of the intermediate tones.
Portative organ. Small portable organ of the late Middle Ages.
Portato (It, pohr-tah'toh). Halfway between legato and staccato.
Pos. Abbr. for Position or for Positif.
Posaune (G, poh-zow'neh). Trombone.
Positif (F). Choir organ.
Position. (1) The point taken by the left hand on the fingerboard of any stringed instrument. (2) Distance apart of the several notes of a chord. (3) Place taken by the slide in trombone playing.
Positive organ. A medium-sized, self-contained medieval organ with one manual and no pedals.
Postlude. Piece played at the conclusion of a service, often improvised.
Potpourri (F, poh-poo-ree'). Medley of all kinds of tunes, or parts of tunes, played in succession, connected by a few measures of introduction or modulation.
Pour (F, poor). For.
Pousseé, poussez (F, poo-say'). Upbow.
Praeambulum (L). Prelude.
Praeludium (L). Prelude.
Precentor. Choir master.
Precipitando (It, preh-chee-pee-tahn'doh). Rushing, impetuous.
Preciso (It, preh-chee'zoh). With precision.
Prelude. Musical introduction to a composition or drama.

Preparation. A dissonant note in a chord is prepared by sounding it as a consonant note in the preceding chord.

Prepared piano. A piano whose sound is changed by the use of various devices such as metal clips or bolts attached to the strings; strips of rubber, felt, paper, etc., inserted across the strings; altered tuning of the unison strings, etc.

Presa (It). The S-shaped sign in canons that indicates the entry point of the various voices.

Pressante (It). Urgent, accelerating.

Prestissimo (It, prehs-tee′see-moh). Very fast.

Presto (It). Fast, rapid.

Prim (G, preem). Prime.

Prima (It, pree′mah). First, principal.

Prima donna (It). Originally the singer of the principal female role in an opera. In the 19th century, the term came to mean a conceited, capricious operatic star.

Prima vista (It). Playing without previous study. Sight reading.

Prima volta, seconda volta (It). First and second endings.

Primary accent. Down-beat.

Primary chords. Most important chords of a Key.

Prime. Interval 'zero', unison.

Primgeiger (G, preem′gy-ger). First violinist, concertmaster.

Primo (It). First or leading part, as in a duet.

Processional. Music played or sung during an entrance.

Program music. Music in which sound is used to depict elements of a story or image in contrast to Absolute music.

Progression. Melodic progression is the advance from one tone to another; harmonic progression is the advance from one chord to another chord.

Prologue. Introductory scene of early operas or ballets.

Prolongement (F, proh-lawn-mahn′). The sostenuto pedal of the piano.

Pronto (It). Promptly, swiftly.

Pronunziato (It, proh-noon-tsee-ah′toh). Pronounced, marked.

Proposta (It, proh-pohs′tah). Subject of a fugue.

Prosa (L), prose (F). Medieval name still in use in France for the sequence.

Psaltery. Type of medieval zither with strings plucked either by the fingers or a plectrum, and related to the Arab qanun.

Psychology of music. Study of the relationship of music to the mind.

Pulse. Beat.

Punta (It, poon'tah). Point of a bow, thrust.

Q

Qanun (kah-noon'). Arab psaltery shaped like a trapezoid and strung with many strings.
Qin (Ch, chin). Chinese seven-stringed zither made of hollowed wood.
Quadrille (F). (1) French dance of the 19th century performed by two or four couples. (2) A square dance.
Quadruple counterpoint. Counterpoint in four parts, all of which may be inverted.
Quadruple fugue. Fugue with four different subjects.
Quadruple time, meter. Four beats to the measure.
Quadruplet. A group of four equal notes played in the time of three notes of the same kind.
Quartal harmony. Harmonic system based on the fourth rather than the common system of the third.
Quarter tone. An interval one-half of a half-step; 24 tones to the octave.
Quartet. Composition for four instruments or four voices; the group of four players or singers.
Quartole (G, kvahr-tohl), **quartolet** (F, kwahr-toh-lay'). Quadruplet.
Quasi (Lat, kwah-zee). As if, nearly.
Quattro (It, kwah'troh). Four.
Quaver. Eighth note.
Quer- (G, kvehr-). Cross, transverse.
Queue (F, kew). The stem of a note.
Quindezime (G). Interval of the 15th, the double octave.
Quint (L), **quinte** (F). Fifth.
Quinta falsa (L). Diminished fifth.
Quintet, quintette. Chamber music for five players.
Quintole (G), **quintolet** (F). Quintuplet.
Quintsaite (G). E string of the violin.
Quintuple meter. A measure of five beats.
Quintuplet. Group of five equal notes played in the time of four notes of the same kind.

Quodlibet

Quodlibet (L, kwahd'lee-beht). Humorous composition in which two or more well-known tunes are sung or played simultaneously.

R

R. Abbr. for Right.
Rabab. Name for various bowed string instruments found in Islamic countries.
Rabbia (It, rahb′bee-ah). Rage, fury, madness.
Raddolcendo (It, rahd-dohl-chen′doh). Becoming softer.
Raddoppiare (It, rahd-dohp-pyah′reh). To double, usually at the lower octave.
Radical bass. Fundamental bass, root of a chord.
Radleyer (G). Hurdy-gurdy.
Raffrenando (It, rahf-frehn-ahn′doh). Slowing down.
Raga. Tonal material for music of India, including scalar pattern and motives. Different ragas are perceived as having different emotional meanings.
Rallentando (It, rahl-lehn-tahn′doh). Gradually slower.
Rank. A complete set of organ pipes of the same type.
Rapidamente (It, rah-pee-dah-mehn′teh). Rapidly.
Rasch (G). Swift, spirited.
Rasgado, rasgueado (S). In guitar playing, strumming the strings with a finger to produce an arpeggio.
Rattenando, rattenuto (It). Holding back.
Rattle. (1) Percussion instrument made of a wooden cogwheel that revolves against a flexible strip of wood or metal. (2) Generic term for shaken idiophones. Many old and widely used instruments are in this category, such as the Latin American maraca, a gourd filled with pebbles or dry seeds and shaken by a wooden handle.
Ravvivando (It, rahv-vee-vahn′doh). Quickening.
Re. Second syllable in Tonic Sol-fa.
Real answer. An answer in a fugue that is an exact (diatonic) transposition of the subject.
Rebab, rebee. Rabab.
Rebec. Ancient stringed instrument.

Recapitulation-Renforcer

Recapitulation. Third section of sonata form following the exposition and the development. It usually contains all the material of the exposition with some modification.

Recessional. Music played or sung at the close of a church service as the choir and clergy leave.

Recht (G). Right.

Récit (F, ray-see). Recitative for solo voice. Solo organ stop.

Recital. Public performance by one or two players in contrast to 'concert' meaning a larger group.

Recitative (F), **recitativo** (It), **rezitativ** (G). Vocal style designed to imitate and emphasize the natural inflections of speech.

Recorder. End-blown flute with a whistle mouthpiece. Usually made in four sizes: soprano, alto, tenor, and bass.

Reco-reco. Native Brazilian scraper made of a gourd or a bamboo cane with carved notches, or a cylindrical metal tube with a piece of corrugated tin fixed to it. It is scraped with a small stick.

Recueilli (F, ruh-koy-yee′). Meditative, contemplative.

Reduction. Arrangement for the piano.

Reed. A thin strip of cane, metal, or other material that is fixed at one end and free to vibrate at the other end.

Refrain. The burden or chorus of a song, usually to be repeated.

Regal. Small portable organ with reed pipes, used during the 16th and 17th centuries.

Register. In an organ, a full set of pipes controlled by one stop.

Registration. The art of using and combining the various stops of the organ.

Related. Term for chords, modes, or Keys that have a close relation of some of their component sounds, thereby making an easy and natural transition from one to another.

Relative pitch. (1) The pitch of a tone in relation to a given Key. (2) The ability to recognize and identify relative pitch. Relative pitch is a requirement for a musician and is considered more important than absolute pitch.

Religioso (It, reh-lee-joh′soh). In a devotional manner.

Remote Key. An unrelated Key.

Renforcer (F, rahn-fohr-say′). To reinforce, to increase in volume.

Renversement-Rigaudon

Renversement (F, rahn-vairs-mahn′). Inversion of intervals, subjects, or chords.
Repeat. Double dotted bar line meaning to repeat a section or division of music.
Repercussion. Repetition of a tone or chord.
Répétition (F), **ripetizione** (It). Rehearsal.
Replica (It). Repeat.
Reprise. Repeat.
Resin. Rosin.
Resolution. The succession of a dissonant note or chord by a consonant note or chord.
Resonance. Transmission of vibrations from a vibrating body to another body.
Resonanzsaiten (G). Sympathetic strings.
Resonator. Any acoustical implement that serves to reinforce sounds by resonance.
Ressortir. To emphasize.
Rest. Silence, pause.
Restatement. Same as recapitulation in sonata form.
Retardation. (1) A holding back, slowing. (2) A suspension resolving upward.
Retrograde. Backward, beginning with the last note and ending with the first note.
Rhapsody. Composition in a free style.
Rhythm. Movement in music with a feeling of regularity and differentiation. Rhythm may be (1) unmetered, as in some types of Asian music; (2) flexible, as in plainsong, where each note is regarded as having approximately the same length; (3) metered, either in rhythmic modes or in a complete system of duple and triple note values.
Rhythmic modes. Thirteenth century system of rhythm which repeats simple rhythm patterns.
Ribibe, ribible. See Rabab.
Ribs. The sides of stringed instruments.
Ricercar, ricercare, ricercata, recercada. Sixteenth and 17th century instrumental composition generally characterized by imitative treatment of the theme or themes.
Ridotto (It, ree-doh′toh). Reduced, arranged.
Riduzione (It, ree-doots-yoh′neh). Arrangement.
Rigaudon, rigadoon. Lively French dance in $\frac{4}{4}$, sometimes $\frac{2}{2}$.

109

Rigo-Rollschweller

Rigo (It, ree′goh). Staff.
Rilasciando (It, ree-lah-shahn′doh). Slowing down.
Rinforzando (It). Abbr. *rf., rfz., rinf.* A sudden accent on a single note or chord.
Ripieno (It, ree-pee-ay′noh). Reinforcing section of the orchestra.
Riposato; riposo, con (It). In a calm, tranquil manner.
Riprendere (It, ree-pren′deh-reh). To resume the original tempo.
Ripresa (It, ree-preh′zah). Repeat. (1) Refrain in the Italian Ballata of the 14th century. (2) Dance movement for lute in the form of a variation in the 16th century. (3) In later music any repeat or recapitulation.
Risoluto (It, ree-soh-loo′toh). Bold, resolute.
Risposta (It, rees-paws′tah). Fugal answer.
Risvegliato (It, rees-vayl-yee-ah′toh). Lively, animated.
Ritardando (It, ree-tahr-dahn′doh). Abbr. rit., ritard. Gradually slower.
Ritenuto (It, ree-teh-noo′toh). Immediate reduction of speed.
Ritmo (It, reet′moh). Rhythm.
Ritornello (It, ree-tawr-nel′loh). The burden of a song; refrain, repeat.
Ritornello form. Term often used for the typical form of the first and sometimes the last movement of the Baroque concerto. It consists of an alternation of Tutti and Solo sections, the Tutti sections being based on the same material while the Solo varies. The Tutti sections form the ritornello.
Riverso, rivolto (It). Terms meaning inversion of intervals, chords or parts; also used to mean retrograde motion.
Robustamente, robusto (It). Firmly and boldly.
Rococo. Eighteenth century ornamental style of architecture and other visual arts, in which elaborate, often delicately executed, ornamentation replaced the massive structure of the Baroque. In music, the pleasant, 'pretty' style referred to sometimes as 'gallant' style.
Rohrblatt (G). The reed of the clarinet, oboe, etc.
Rohrstimmen (G, rohr-shtim′men), **Rohrwerk** (G, rohr′vairk). The reed of an organ.
Rollschweller (G). The crescendo pedal of the organ.

Romance, romanze, romanza. Originally a ballad or popular tale in verse. Now a title for songs or short instrumental pieces of a lyrical character.

Romantic music, Romanticism. In literature and all the Arts, a movement from about 1820 to 1910 away from the restrictions imposed by Classicism toward greater freedom of form, with emphasis on subjective, emotional qualities. Three major contributions to music of this period were the 'character piece' for piano, the 'art song' for voice and piano, and the 'symphonic poem' for orchestra.

Ronde (F). Whole note.

Rondeau. (1) Form of medieval French poetry and music; (2) Instrumental form of the 17th century consisting of a repeated refrain and different couplets, A B A C A D A.

Rondelet. Roundelay.

Rondo, rondo form. Composition consisting of a main theme which reappears again and again alternating with contrasting themes.

Root. The fundamental note of any chord.

Rosin, resin. The substance applied to bows of stringed instruments to increase traction.

Rota. Round.

Rote. Fixed mechanical way of doing something; routine. By rote, by memory alone, without understanding or thought.

Rotta, rotte, rota. (1) Medieval instrument similar to the psaltery; (2) In 14th century Italian dances, an after-dance that is a rhythmic variant of the main dance.

Roulade (F, roo-lahd'). An ornamental vocal or instrumental passage.

Round. Common name for a circle canon. A composition in which three or more parts (a) enter in succession with the same music and words, (b) sing as many phrases as there are parts, and (c) return to the first phrase. The phrases are of equal length and written so as to make harmony.

Roundelay. Rondeau, rondelet.

Rovescio (It, roh-vehs'chee-oh). Retrograde motion or inversion.

Row. Same as *tone row*.

Rubab. Rabab.

Rubato (It, roo-bah'toh). A flexible, elastic tempo that has slight accelerandos and ritardandos that alternate according to the needs of musical expression.
Run. A rapid scale passage.
Rustico (It, roo'stee-koh). Rural, pastoral.

S

S. Abbr. for Segno, Senza, Sinistra, Solo, Soprano, Sordini, Subito.
Saccadé (F, sah-kah-day′). Abrupt, jerky.
Sackbut. Early form of trombone.
Sackpfeife (G, zahk′pfyf-uh). Bagpipe.
Saite (G, zy′tuh). A string.
Saltando, saltato (It). Leaping, proceeding by skips or jumps. In string playing, indicates that the bow is to bounce lightly on the string.
Salterio (It, S). Psaltery, dulcimer.
Sanft (G). Soft, gentle.
Sans (F, sahn). Without.
Saraband, sarabande. Seventeenth and 18th century dance that was regularly included in the Suite between 1650 and 1750. In slow triple meter, it is usually without an upbeat, frequently with an accent or prolonged tone on the second beat, and with feminine endings of the phrases.
Sarrusophone. Brass wind instrument with a double reed, named for its French inventor, Sarrus, around 1856.
Sassofone (It). Saxophone.
Satz (G). (1) Movement, as of a sonata or symphony. (2) In composition, 'style'.
Sautillé (F, soh-tee-yay). In violin playing, a short stroke of the bow played in a rapid tempo in the middle of the bow so that the bow bounces slightly off the string.
Saxophone. Family of instruments invented by Adolphe Sax of Brussels in the 19th century. They are played with a single beating reed, as are the clarinets, but are conical in bore as are the oboes. The key mechanism and fingering resemble those of the clarinet.
Scala (It, skah′lah). Scale.

Scale-Scucito

Scale. (1) The tonal material of music arranged in an order of ascending and descending pitches. See pages 10–13. (2) In pipe organs, the ratio between length and width of pipes; in the piano, the ratio between length and thickness of strings and method of tuning.
Schalkhaft (G). Roguish, sportive.
Schall (G, shahl). Sound, chiefly acoustical.
Scherzando (It, skehr-tsahn'doh), **scherzhaft** (G, skehrts'hahft). In a playful manner.
Scherzo (It, skehrts'oh). A joke, jest. (1) A piece of lively, humorous character. (2) A movement in sonatas, symphonies, and quartets.
Schiettamente (It, skee-eht-tah-mehn'teh). Simply, openly.
Schlag (G, shlahkh). A beat or stroke.
Schlagzither (G). Modern plucked zither in contrast to earlier bowed zithers.
Schlegel (G, shlay'gl). Drumstick.
Schleppend (G). Dragging, heavy.
Schlummerlied (G). Slumber song.
Schluss (G, shloos). End, cadence.
Schlüssel (G, shleesl). Clef.
Schnarre (G). Rattle.
Schnell (G). Fast.
Schottische (G). Round dance similar to a polka.
Schrittmässig (G). Measured.
Schwingung (G, shving-oong). Vibration.
Schwungvoll (G). Animated, spirited.
Sciolto (It, shee-ohl'toh). Easily, freely.
Scordatura (It, skohr-dah-too'rah). Unusual tuning of a stringed instrument in order to obtain unusual chords, facilitate difficult passages, or change the tone color.
Score. Notation showing all parts of an ensemble arranged one beneath the other on different staves. Vocal score usually shows all the vocal parts on separate staves. A piano score is the reduction of an orchestral score to a version for piano alone.
Scorrendo (It, skohr-rehn'doh), **scorrevole** (It, skohr-ray'voh-leh). Flowing, gliding.
Scucito (It, skoo-chee'toh). Unconnected, non-legato.

Segno-Shake

Segno (It, sayn'yoh). Sign used to indicate the beginning or end or a section to be repeated. [𝄋]
Segue (It, say'gweh). Instruction to the performer to play the following movement without a break.
Sehr (G, zayr). Very.
Semi (L). Half.
Semibreve. Half a breve. British name for a whole note.
Semitone. Half step.
Semplice (It, sehm'plee-chay). Simple, unaffected.
Sempre (It, sehm'pray). Always, evermore.
Sentimento (It, sayn-tee-mehn'toh). With feeling, sentiment.
Sentito It, sehn-tee'toh). Expressive.
Senza (It, sen'tsah). Without.
Septet. Composition for seven voices or instruments.
Septuplet. A group of seven equal notes played in the time of four or six notes of the same value.
Sequence. Repetition of the same melodic pattern at a different pitch.
Serenade. Evening music, instrumental or vocal.
Serenata (It). (1) Serenade. (2) Eighteenth century short opera or cantata.
Sereno (It, say-ray'noh). Serene, calm.
Serial music. Compositional technique in which thematic materials are derived from a series of all twelve notes of the chromatic scale. Serialism may also extend to other elements such as rhythm, dynamics, and timbre.
Sestetto (It). Sextet.
Seventh chord. A chord consisting of the third, fifth, and seventh above the fundamental. See pages 9–10.
Sextet. A composition for six voices or for six instruments, or the group of six performers.
Sextole (L, sex'toh-lay). Sextuplet.
Sextuplet. A group of six equal notes played in the time of four notes of the same value. Notation should indicate whether the six notes are meant to form three groups of two each, or two groups of three each.
Sforzando (It, sfohr-tsahn'doh). Abbr. [sfz] Sudden strong accent on a single note or chord.
Sforzato (It, sfohr-tsah'toh). Sforzando.
Shake. Old name for the trill.

Shanty-Sino

Shanty, chanty, chantey. Work song of English and American sailors.
Sharp. [♯] Musical note or tone one-half step higher than the tone named.
Sharp, double. [x] Sign which means to raise the pitch of a note one whole step.
Sheng. Chinese free-reed mouth organ with bamboo pipes of different lengths fitted to a gourd. It is played by alternately inhaling and exhaling.
Sho. Japanese name for *sheng*.
Shift. A change of position of the left hand in playing a string instrument.
Shofar. Ancient Jewish instrument made from a ram's horn.
Si (It, F, see). Syllable for the seventh tone of a diatonic scale.
Siciliana, siciliano. Seventeenth and 18th century dance of Sicilian origin in moderate § or ⁱ²⁄₈ time. Slow, soothing, pastoral character.
Sight reading, sight singing. Reading and performing music at sight without previous preparation.
Signature. Sign placed at the beginning of a composition indicating the Key (see *Key Signature*) or meter (see *Time Signature*).
Signs. See pages 14–15.
Similar motion. Two or more parts ascending or descending at the same time.
Simile (It, see-mee-lay). In the same way.
Sin al fine (It). To the end.
Sinfonia (It). (1) Symphony. (2) Name chosen by J. S. Bach for his Three Part Inventions. (3) An opera overture.
Sinfonia concertante (It). Eighteenth century term for a symphony with one or more solo instruments.
Sinfonietta (It). Small symphony orchestra.
Singing saw. Musical saw.
Singspiel (G, zing'shpeel). A type of German opera of the 18th century. It was usually light and included spoken dialogue.
Sinistra (It, see-nee'strah). Left (hand).
Sino (It, see'noh). To; as far as; until.

Sitar-Solfegietto

Sitar. Well-known stringed instrument of India. It usually has five melodic strings and two drone strings. Under these strings are thirteen strings that vibrate sympathetically with the strings being plucked.
Six-four chord. The second inversion of a triad.
Sixth tone. Interval equal to one-third of a half step; 36 sixth tones to the octave.
Skala (G). Scale.
Skip. Melodic progression by an interval wider than a second.
Slancio, con (It, kohn slahn'tshee-oh). With dash, impetuously.
Slargando (It, slahr-gahn'doh). Slowing down.
Slentando (It, slehn-tahn'doh). Slackening, slowing down.
Slide. (1) The movable part of the trombone. (2) A rapid ornament of two or three sale tones. (3) In violin playing, a slight 'portamento' used to pass quickly from one note to another.
Slur. A curved line over or under two or more notes indicating that they are to be played legato. In violin playing, one stroke of the bow; in singing, one breath.
Sminuendo (It, smeen-oo-ehn'doh). Same as Diminuendo.
Smorzando (It, smohr-tsahn'doh). Fading away.
Snare drum. Side drum with two heads stretched over a metal shell. The upper head is struck with two drumsticks and is called the 'batter head'. Gut or silk strings called 'snares' are stretched across the lower head or 'snare head'. The vibrations of the snares against this head create a brilliant tone quality.
Snello (It). Nimble, agile.
Soave (It, soh-ah'vay). Gentle, sweet.
Sociology of music. Study of the relationship between music and society.
Soggetto (It, sohd-jet'toh). Subject, theme.
Sol. Fifth syllable in Tonic Sol-fa.
Sol-fa. English method of solmization for the purpose of sight singing.
Solfège (F, sohl-fezh), **solfeggio** (It, sohl-fed'jee-oh). (1) Vocal exercises sung to vowels or to the syllables of solmization. (2) Instruction in the rudiments of music.
Solfegietto (It, sohl-feh-jeh'toh). Title used by some composers to mean 'little study'.

Solmization-Sound holes

Solmization. Term for systems of naming the degrees of the scale by syllables instead of letters. The syllables most used are do, re, mi, fa, sol, la, ti (si).
Solo (It). Alone. A composition for a single voice or instrument.
Solo pitch. Pitch slightly higher than normal; used occasionally to obtain a brilliant tone.
Son (F, sohn). Sound, tone.
Sonata. An instrumental composition in three or four movements, usually for a solo instrument.
Sonata form. Term that refers to a pattern of composition used for the first movements of sonatas, symphonies, quartets, concertos, etc. They usually consist of three main sections: exposition, development, and recapitulation.
Sonatina. Short Sonata.
Song. Short composition for solo voice.
Song cycle. Group of related songs that form a musical entity.
Song form. Simple A B A ternary form.
Sonido trece (S). Name used by 20th century composer Julián Carrillo for his method of using microtonic intervals. He used $1/3$, $1/4$, $1/8$, and $1/16$ whole tones on pianos and harps of his own manufacture in Mexico.
Sonore (F, soh-nohr). Sonorous, with full tone.
Sopra (It, soh'prah). Above, upon, over.
Soprano. Highest female voice.
Sordino (It, sohr-dee'noh). Mute.
Sospirando (It, sohs-pee-rahn'doh). Sighing, plaintive.
Sostenuto, sostenendo (It). Sustaining the tone, giving full duration.
Sostenuto pedal. The third pedal on some pianos, usually grand, that sustains only those tones whose dampers are already raised by the action of the keys. It permits the sustaining of singing notes while both hands are occupied elsewhere and provides for various coloristic effects.
Sotto (It, soh'toh). Below, under.
Soubrette (F, soo-breht'uh). Light, operatic soprano.
Soundboard. In pianos, the wooden surface over which the strings are stretched. It serves as a resonator.
Sound holes. Openings of various shapes cut in the table, or top, of stringed instruments.

Sound post-Stil

Sound post. In the violin family, a small wooden prop set between the table and the back.
Soupirant (F). Sighing, plaintive.
Sourd, sourde (F). Muffled, muted.
Sousaphone. Tuba made in a circular shape so that it may be carried on the player's shoulders.
Sp. Abbr. for Spitze.
Space. The interval between any two lines of the staff or between any two leger lines.
Speaker key. In wind instruments, a key that opens a small hole at a point that aids the playing of the octave, 12th, and 13th.
Speaking stop. On organs, a stop that produces sounds in contrast to one that only operates couplers, etc.
Sperdendosi (It, spair-dehn-doh'zee). Fading away.
Spezzato (It, sped-zah'toh). Divided.
Spianato (It spee-ah-nah'toh). Smooth, even.
Spiccato (It, spee-kah-toh). Separated, detached.
Spieldose (G, shpeel'doh-zeh). Music box.
Spinet. Small harpsichord or small piano.
Spiritoso (It, spee-ree-toh'soh). With spirit, animation.
Spiritual. Genre of American religious folk song popularized during the 1800s.
Spitze (G, shpeet'suh). Point; in violin playing, point of bow; in organ playing, the toe.
Sprechstimme, Sprechgesang (G). Intoned voice production halfway between song and speech.
Staccato (It). Detached, separated. Indicated by small dots or wedge marks over or under the notes.
Staff. The five horizontal lines used in modern music notation (plural, 'staves').
Ständchen (G, stend'khen). Serenade.
Steg (G, shtekh). Bridge of the violin.
Stegreif (G, shtekh-rife). Improvisation, performance without preparation.
Stendando (It, stehn-tahn'doh). Slowing down.
Step. Progression of a second.
Steso (It, steh'zoh). Slow.
Stesso (It, stes'soh). The same.
Stil (G, shteel), **stile** (It, stee'lay), **stilo** (It, stee-loh). Style.

119

Stimm-Stromentato

Stimm (G, shtim). Having to do with voice, part, tone.
Stimme (G, shtim′meh). (1) The voice; (2) voice part.
Stimmung (G). Tuning, intonation.
Stinguendo (It, steen-gwen′doh). Dying away.
Stirato (It, stee-rah′toh). Drawing out, slowing down.
Stop. (1) Mechanical device in the organ by which the player draws on or shuts off the various registers. (2) On the violin, the pressure of the finger upon the string. (3) In the harpsichord, chromatic sets of strings corresponding to the keys of the keyboard. Stops have various pitch levels and tone colors.
Straff (G, shtrahf). Rigid, firm.
Straziante (It, strahts-yahn′teh). Anguished.
Streich- (G, strike). Bow.
Strepitoso (It, streh-pee-toh′zoh). Noisy, boisterous.
Stretta (It, streht′tah). Concluding passage in a faster tempo than the preceding passage.
Stretto (It, streh-toh). (1) In a fugue, the imitation of the answer in close succession, with the answer entering before the subject is completed. This overlapping produces an increased intensity that concludes the fugue with a climax. (2) Same as stretta in non-fugal works.
Strich (G, shtreekh). Bow strike.
Stringed instruments. Instruments that produce tones when their strings are struck, plucked, or bowed.
String quartet. Chamber music for four stringed instruments, usually the first and second violins, viola, and cello; or the four performers.
String quintet. Composition for five stringed instruments, or the group itself.
Strings. Colloquial abbreviation for the stringed instruments of the orchestra.
String trio. Composition for three stringed instruments of the orchestra.
Strisciando (It, stree-shahn′doh). Correct Italian term for Glissando.
Stroboconn. Electronic-stroboscopic frequency meter used to measure acoustical frequencies.
Stromento (It, stroh-mehn′toh). Instrument.
Stromentato (It, stroh-men-tah′toh). Played by instruments.

Stück (G). A piece, composition.
Stufe (G, shtoo′fuh). Degree of the scale.
Style. Mode of expression or performance. In composition, the methods of treating the elements of form, melody, rhythm, etc.
Style galant (F, steel gah-lahn′). Gallant style.
Sub (L). Under, below, beneath.
Subdominant. The fourth degree of an ascending scale; a fifth below the Tonic.
Subito (It, soo′bee-toh). Suddenly, at once.
Subject. Melodic theme or motive.
Submediant. The sixth degree of an ascending scale; a third below the Tonic.
Suboctave. The octave below a given part.
Subtonic. The seventh degree of an ascending scale; usually one whole step below the Tonic.
Suite (F, sweet). A series of pieces.
Sul, sull', sulla, sulle (It). On, upon.
Superdominant. The sixth degree of an ascending scale.
Supertonic. The second degree of an ascending scale.
Suspension. The sustaining of one of the notes of a consonant interval while the other notes move so that the interval becomes dissonant. The dissonance is then resolved.
Sussurando (It, soo-soo-rahn′doh). Whispering, murmuring.
Svelto (It, svel-toh). Quick, nimble.
Svolgimento (It, svoh-lee-mehn′toh). Development.
Swell. Gradual increase in volume.
Swell organ (F, recit; G, Oberwerk). The upper manual and the pipes it controls. The pipes are enclosed in a box with shutters that may be opened and closed.
Sympathetic string. String that is not being played, but by vibrating along with the plucked or bowed strings reinforces the sound of them.
Sympathetic vibrations. Vibrations created in a body by the action of the vibrations of another body.
Symphony. An extended composition for orchestra, usually having from three to five movements.
Syncopation. Generally any deliberate disturbance of the normal pulse of rhythm, meter, and accent.

Synthesizer

Synthesizer. Twentieth century electronic instrument which uses filters and oscillators or digital circuitry to produce sounds unobtainable from conventional musical instruments.

T

T. Abbr. for Tasto, Tempo, Tenor, Toe, Trill, Tonic, and Tutti.
Tablature. Various systems of notation usually for lute or guitar that use letters, numbers, or other signs to indicate which strings or frets are to be played.
Tacet. Direction to be silent. The term is found in orchestral scores for parts not needed for a movement or a long section.
Takt (G, tahkt). Beat; a measure; time.
Talon (F, tah-lohn'). Nut of the violin bow.
Tambora (S). Any of several two-headed drums found throughout Latin America.
Tambour (F, tahm-boor). Drum; a drummer.
Tambourin (tam'boo-rin). Small, two-headed medieval drum, cylindrical in shape, with both heads covered with skin.
Tambourine (tam-boo-reen'). Small, shallow single-headed drum with metal disks inserted into the wooden shell. Usually it is played by striking with the hand or by shaking.
Tambur. Name for any of several lutes found from the Balkan Peninsula throughout the Middle East.
Tambura. Long-necked, unfretted, round-bodied drone lute of India. It has four metal strings that are plucked with one finger.
Tamburin (G), **tamburino** (It). Usually the modern tambourine.
Tamburo (It). Drum, kettledrum.
Tampon. Two-headed drumstick used to produce a roll on the bass drum.
Tamtam. Gong of indefinite pitch.
Tanbur. See tambur.
Tangent. Brass blade that strikes the strings of the clavichord.

Tango-Terzina

Tango (S). Argentinean dance performed by couples. The music usually consists of two sections of equal length with the second generally in the Dominant or Relative minor of the original Key. The rhythm is based on syncopated patterns within a $\frac{2}{4}$ meter.
Tanz (G, tahnts). Dance.
Tarantella. Italian dance in rapid $\frac{6}{8}$ meter.
Tardamente (It, tahr-dah-mehn'tay). Slowly.
Tardando (G, tahr-dahn'doh). Slowing down.
Tardo (It, tahr'doh). Slow, lingering.
Tastiera (It, tahs-tee-eh'rah). Keyboard.
Tasto (It, tah'stoh). Key of a keyboard.
Tasto solo. In old music, bass notes only, no accompaniment.
Technic. The skill of playing an instrument or singing.
Tema (It, tay'mah). Theme.
Temperament. Division of the octave into twelve equal tones, half-steps.
Tempestoso (It, tehm-peh-stoh'soh). Stormily, passionately.
Tempo. Speed of a composition or section.
Tempo marks. Words or phrases to indicate the rate of speed at which a piece should be performed. See pages 18–19.
Temps (F, tahm). Beat.
Ten. Abbr. for Tenuto.
Teneramente (It, teh-neh-rah-men'teh). Tenderly, softly, delicately.
Tenor. (1) Highest male voice. (2) Before names of instruments, indicates tenor range, as 'tenor horn'. (3) Second lowest part in four-part writing.
Tenor C. Second space C of the bass clef.
Tenor clef. The C clef on the 4th line of the staff.
Tenth. An interval of one octave plus two degrees.
Tenuto (It, teh-noo'toh). Sustained, held full time.
Ternary form. Consists of three main sections. Usually called 'A B A form'.
Tertian harmony. Western system of harmony based on the interval of a third.
Terz (G, tairts). Third.
Terzett (G, tair-tseht'), **terzetto** (It, tair-tseh'toh). Vocal trio.
Terzina (It, tair-tseen'ah). Triplet.

Tessitura - Timpani

Tessitura (It, tehs-see-too'rah). General range of a vocal part, not including a few isolated high or low notes.

Testo (It). Narrator in oratorios, passions, etc.

Tetrachord. Lit. 'that which has four strings'. A segment of the scale of Ancient Greek music consisting of four notes descending through a perfect fourth. In general usage, four scale tones contained in a perfect fourth.

Text. Words to which music is set.

Theme. (1) The main idea in a composition. (2) The subject in the development of a sonata or of a fugue. (3) A simple tune on which variations are made.

Theory of music. The understanding of the fundamentals of music such as notation, harmony, counterpoint, rhythm, melody, intervals, scales, etc.

Theremin. An electronic instrument named for the Russian scientist who invented it about 1924.

Thesis (G, thay'sis). Downbeat.

Thorough bass, figured bass. A bass with numerals placed over or under the notes to indicate harmony.

Thunder machine. A large rotating drum containing hard balls that simulate the sound of thunder as they strike against the drumhead. Introduced in 1915 by R. Strauss.

Tie. A curved line that connects two notes on the same line or space. Only the first note is played and is then held for the value of both notes.

Timbale (F), **timballo, timpano** (It). Kettledrum.

Timbre (F, tan'br). Tone quality.

Timbrel. Tambourine.

Time. General term that means tempo, meter, or duration of notes.

Time Signature. Two numerals at the beginning of a piece or section indicating the number of beats in each measure and the kind of note receiving one beat.

Timing. The duration or length of a performance; used particularly in radio, television, and recording.

Timoroso (It, tee-moh-roh'soh). Timidly, with hesitation.

Timpán. Medieval Irish plucked stringed instrument of the psaltery type; later more like the dulcimer, with a rod to strike the strings.

Timpani (It, teem'pah-nee). Kettledrums.

Tiple-Tonleiter

Tiple (S). Upper voice, soprano.
Tirare (It, tee-rah'reh). To draw.
Toccata (It, tohk-kah'tah; from *toccare* meaning 'to touch'). Generally a piece with a flowing movement of notes of equal value; usually for a keyboard instrument.
Todeslied (G, toh'des-leet'). A dirge or funeral song.
Tom-tom. A pair of tuned drums.
Ton (G, tohn; F, tawn). Tone, sound, pitch, Key, mode.
Tonabstand (G, tohn-ahp'shtant). Interval.
Tonal. Pertaining to tone, mode, or Key.
Tonality. The organization of a series of notes or chords to a focal point which becomes the tonal center of the composition. The tonal center is called the 'Tonic'.
Tonart (G). Key, scale, mode.
Tondichtung (G, tohn'dikh-toong). Tone poem, symphonic poem.
Tone. (1) A given, fixed sound of a certain pitch and duration. (2) Interval of a Major second, a whole tone.
Tone cluster. Group of tones on a keyboard played simultaneously with the forearm, fist, or elbow.
Tone color. Quality of tone.
Tone poem. Nineteenth and 20th century orchestral composition based on a poetic or programmatic idea rather than on a musical one.
Tone row. See *Twelve-tone technique.*
Tonette. A small end-blown flute with finger holes.
Tonguing. In wind instruments, the use of the tongue for articulation. *Single tonguing* is used for nearly all the wind instruments. *Double* and *triple tonguing* is used mostly for brass instruments and the flute.
Tonhöhe (G). Pitch.
Tonic. The tonal center or keynote of a composition. The first note of a scale.
Tonic sol-fa. English method of solmization. The tones are sung to syllables and the ear is trained to recognized intervals. It uses a moveable Do.
Tonika (G, toh'nee-kah). Tonic.
Tonkunst (G, tohn-koonst). Music.
Tonkünstler (G, tohn-keenst-lair). Composer.
Tonleiter (G, tohn'lye-tair). Scale.

Tonmalerei-Tremolo

Tonmalerei (G, tohn-mahl'air-eye). Descriptive music.
Tono (It, toh'noh). (1) Tone. (2) Whole tone. (3) Key.
Tonsatz (G, tohn'zahtz). A composition.
Tonschrift (G, tohn'shrift). Notation.
Tonus (L). Whole tone.
Tosto (It, toh'stoh). Quickly, at once.
Touch. The manner in which a key on a keyboard is depressed.
Touche (F, toosh). (1) Keyboard of a piano. (2) Fingerboard of a stringed instrument.
Toye. Short piece for the virginal.
Tracker action. In pipe organs, the mechanical system of key action.
Tranquillo (It, trahn-kweel'loh). Calmly, tranquilly, quietly.
Transcription. Arrangement or adaptation of a piece of music for a voice or instrument other than that for which it was originally composed.
Transient. Passing, not principal.
Transition. (1) A transient modulation. (2) passing suddenly from one key to another. (3) a passage leading from one theme to another.
Transposition. The changing of a composition into a key other than the key in which it was originally written.
Transposing instruments. Instruments whose music is written in a key other than their actual sounds.
Trascinando (It, trah-shee-nahn-doh). Dragging, slowing.
Trattenuto (It, traht-teh-noo'toh). Delayed, slowing down.
Trauermusik (G, trow'er-moo-zeek'). Funeral music.
Träumerisch (G, troy'mehrish). Dreamy.
Tre (It, tray). Three.
Treble. The highest part; soprano.
Treble clef. The G clef.
Tre corde (It, tray kohr'deh). Three strings. In piano music, direction to release the soft pedal.
Treibend (G, try-bent). Hurrying.
Tremando (It, treh-mahn'doh). With a tremolo effect.
Tremolo. A quivering, fluttering. (1) On stringed instruments, an effect produced by the rapid alternation of an up and down bow. (2) In singing, an unsteady tone. (3) On the piano, the rapid alternation of chord tones or octaves. (4) On the pipe organ, the use of the tremulant stop.

Tremulant-Tuning

Tremulant. An organ stop that produces a tremolo effect.
Trepak (treh'pahk). Cossack dance in quick, duple time.
Très (F, treh). Very, molto.
Triad. Any chord of three notes composed of a root, third, and fifth.
Triangle. Percussion instrument made of a small cylindrical piece of steel bent into a triangular shape. It is struck with a metal rod.
Tricesimoprimal temperament. Division of the octave into 31 equal tones.
Trill, Triller (G), **trillo** (It). An ornament consisting of the rapid alternation of two adjacent tones.
Trinklied (G, trink'leet). Drinking song.
Trio. (1) A composition for three voices or three instruments. (2) A contrasting section in minuets, marches, gavottes, etc. (3) A group of three performers.
Triole (G), **triolet** (F). Triplet.
Trio sonata. A type of Baroque chamber music written in three parts, the two upper parts supported by a figured bass.
Triplet. A group of three equal notes played in the time of two notes of the same value.
Tritone. The interval of three whole steps, the augmented fourth or diminished fifth.
Tromba (It). Trumpet, bugle.
Trombone. Brass instrument, with a U-shaped slide in place of valves, and a flaring bell. It provides the tenor voice of the brass family.
Trommel (G, trah'mel). Drum.
Troppo (It, trohp'poh). Too, too much. *Allegro, ma non troppo,* fast, but not too fast.
Troubadours. Twelfth century poet-musicians of Provence and North France.
Trumpet. Brass instrument with mouthpiece, metal tube, and small bell. It has a brilliant, penetrating tone quality.
Tuba. General name for bass-pitched brass instruments other than the trombones.
Tubaphone. Percussion instrument similar to the glockenspiel. Lengths of metal pipe produce its sounds.
Tune. Air, melody.
Tuning. The process of bringing an instrument into tune.

Tuning fork-Tympani

Tuning fork. A small two-pronged steel fork used to indicate absolute pitch.
Turca, alla (It, ahl-lah toor'kah). In the Turkish style.
Turn. An ornament consisting of four or five notes that turn around the principal note.
Tusch (G, toosh). A fanfare played on brass instruments.
Tutti (It, toot'tee). All, whole. It is usually used in concertos to indicate the whole orchestra.
Twelfth. Interval of an octave plus a fifth.
Twelve-tone technique. A consecutive arrangement (series) of the twelve half-steps of the chromatic octave, used in the composition of serial music. All twelve tones of the octave have equal importance. Once begun, all twelve tones of the series must be used before the series can begin again.
Tympani (It, teem'pah-nee). Kettledrums.

U

Über- (G). Over, above.
Übung (G). Exercise, study.
Uguale (It, oo-gwah′leh). Equal, uniform.
Ukulele. Small stringed instrument of the guitar family with four strings and a long, fretted fingerboard.
Umfang (G, oom′fahng). Compass, range.
Umkehrung (G, oom′kehr-oong). Inversion.
Umstimmen (G, oom′shtim-men). Tuning change, as in kettledrums.
Un, una, uno (It). A, an, one.
Una corda (It, oo′nah kor′dah). One string. On the piano, direction to use the soft pedal.
Undezime (G, oon-dehts′ee-may). Eleventh.
Unequal temperament. Any system of tuning between pure intonation and equal temperament.
Unequal voices. Mixture of men's and women's voices.
Ungebunden (G, oon′geh-boon′dehn). Free, unrestrained.
Unison. The sounding of the same note or pitch by two or more instruments or voices. On the piano, three strings tuned to the same pitch are called a unison.
Unter- (G, oon-tair). Under, below, sub.
Upbeat. (1) the raising of the conductor's hand. (2) Unaccented part of the measure.
Up-bow. [∨] Stroke of the bow in the direction from point to nut.
Ut (Lat, F, oot). (1) First of the solmization syllables. (2) In France, the note C.
Ut supra (L). As before, as above.

V

V. Abbr. for Vide, Violin, Voce, and Volti.
Va (It, vah). Go on, continue.
Vaghezza, con (It, kohn vah-geht′tsah). With charm, grace.
Vago (It, vah′goh). Vague, dreamy.
Valse. Waltz.
Valve. In brass wind instruments, a device for directing the air current from the main tube into a side tube. This lengthens the air column and lowers the pitch of the entire scale so that all chromatic tones are available.
Vamp. Improvised accompaniment used in popular music.
Variations. A musical form in which a theme is developed into a series of variations by means of harmonic, rhythmic, melodic, and other changes.
Varsovienne. Polish dance in moderate $\frac{3}{4}$ time.
Velato (It, vay-lah′toh). Veiled.
Vellutato (It, vehl-loo-tah′toh). Velvety.
Veloce (It, veh-loh′chay). Swiftly, fast.
Vent (F, vahn). Wind.
Ventil (G, fehn′till), **ventile** (It, vehn-tee′leh). Valve.
Vergrösserung (G). Augmentation.
Verhallend (G, fair-hahl′ent). Fading away.
Verkleinerung (G, fair-kline′air-oong). Diminution.
Vermindert (G, fair-min′dairt). Diminished, as an interval.
Verschiebung (G, fair-sheeb′oong). Soft pedal.
Verschwinden (G, fair-shvin′dehn). Fading away, vanishing.
Versetzung (G, fair-zehts′oong). Transposition.
Vezzoso (It, veht-tsoh′zoh). Graceful, elegant.
Via (It, vee′ah). Away.
Vibraharp, vibraphone. Percussion instrument on which tuned metal bars in the keyboard patterns are struck with small hammers. Resonators below the bars open and close electrically producing a vibrato.

Vibrato-Voce

Vibrato. Rapid fluctuations of pitch. (1) On stringed instruments, produced by rapid oscillations of the left hand on the stopped string. (2) In singing, a tremulous effect caused by very rapid partial interruptions of the tone.

Vide (L). Written in scores, it means that an omission is to be made; directs the performers to skip from *Vi-* to *de.*

Viel (G, feel). Much, great.

Vielstimmig (G, feel'shtim-mikh). Polyphonic, for many voices.

Viertel (G, feer-tehl). Quarter.

Vif (F, veef). Lively.

Vigoroso (It, vee-goh-roh'soh). With vigor, energy.

Vina. Important stringed instrument of India.

Viol. Name for a family of bowed stringed instruments of the 16th and 17th centuries. Three sizes were normally used in chamber music: treble, tenor, and bass.

Viola (It, vee-oh'lah). Stringed instrument of the violin family, slightly larger than the violin and tuned a fifth lower.

Viola da gamba. Bass of the viol family.

Viole (F, vayawl). Viol, viola.

Violento (It, vee-oh-lehn'toh). Violently.

Violin. Familiar four-stringed bowed instrument; the leading instrument of the orchestra; the highest pitched member of the violin family.

Violin family. Violin, viola, cello, and double bass.

Violoncello (It, vee-oh-lon-tchel'loh). Same as cello.

Violone (It, vee-oh-loh'neh). Largest size of the viol.

Virginal. Small harpsichord.

Virtuoso. Highly skilled performer.

Vista (It, vee'stah). Sight. *A prima vista,* at sight.

Vite, vitement (F, veet, veet-mahn'). Fast, swiftly.

Vivace (It, vee-vah'chay). Lively, animated.

Vivo (It, vee'voh). Briskly, lively.

Vocal. Pertaining to the voice.

Vocalise (F, voh-kah-leez). Vocal exercise.

Vocalize. To practice vocal exercise.

Voce (It, voh'chay). Voice.

Voice-Vuoto

Voice. The human instrument that produces the sounds of singing and speaking. The singing voice is usually classified *bass, baritone, tenor, alto, mezzo-soprano,* or *soprano.* The word is also used for 'Part' in composition and for 'range' in describing instruments.

Voicing. On the organ, tuning. On the piano, the adjustment of the hammer felts to produce the desirable tone quality.

Voix (F, vwah). Voice.

Volante (It, voh-lahn'teh). Flying, rushing.

Volata (It), **Volate** (G), **volatine** (F). Rapid series of notes.

Volkslied (G, fohlks'leet). Folk song.

Voll (Gk fohl). Full.

Volteggiando (It, vohl-tehd-jahn'doh). Crossing the hands on a keyboard.

Volti subito (It). Abbr. 'V.S.' Turn the page over quickly.

Vorausnahme (G, fohr-ows'nah-meh). Anticipation.

Vordersatz (G, fohr'dair-zatz). First subject.

Vorhalt (G, fohr'halt). Suspension.

Vorschlag (G, fohr'shlakh). Appoggiatura.

Vorspiel (G, fohr'shpeel). Prelude, overture, introduction.

Vortrag (G, fohr'tragh). Execution, interpretation, performance.

Vortragszeichen (G, fohr-trag-tsyk'en). Expression marks.

Vorwärts (G, fohr'varts). Continue, go ahead.

Vorzeichnung (G, fohr-tsyk'noong). Both Key and Time Signature.

Vox (L). Human voice.

Vuoto (It, vwoh'toh). Empty. *Corda vuota,* open string.

W

Wachsend (G, vahks'ent). Increasing, growing.
Waldhorn (G, vahlt'horn). French horn.
Waltz. Dance in ¾ time that varies from moderate to fast speed.
Wärme, mit (G, mit vair'muh). With warmth.
Wehmütig (G, vay'mewt-igh). Sad, melancholy.
Weich (G, vyk). Soft, gentle.
Weihnachtsmusik (G, vy'nakhts-moo'zik). Christmas music.
Whistle. Small end-blown pipe.
Whole note. Semibreve.
Whole step. Interval of a Major second. Two half-steps.
Whole tone. Whole step.
Whole tone scale. Scale consisting only of whole tones.
Wind instruments. General name for all instruments whose tone is produced by compressed air.
Wind machine. A barrel framework covered with cloth. It is rotated so that the cloth rubs against cardboard or wood and simulates the sound of wind.
Wolf (G, voolf). (1) Discord resulting from imperfect tuning. (2) The slight difference in pitch between enharmonic tones in the mean tone system. (3) In string playing, a discordant sound produced by a faulty string or jarring vibration.
Woodwinds. (1) Orchestral instruments generally made of wood. (2) Woodwind players.
Wuchtig (G, vooch'tig). Heavy, ponderously.
Würdig (G, voor'digh). Dignified, stately.

X

Xylophone. Tuned percussion instrument made of wooden bars that are struck with small, hard-headed sticks. The bars are arranged like a keyboard with a resonator under each bar.

Y

Yodel. Alpine song and style of singing characterized by rapid alternate passings between falsetto and chest tones.

Yueqin. Chinese short-necked lute with round sound box and four strings.

Z

Zählzeit (G, tsail'tsight). Beat.
Zampogna (It, tsahm-pohn-yah). Mouth-blown bagpipe.
Zanfona (S). Hurdy-gurdy.
Zart (G, tsart). Tender, soft, delicate.
Zeitmass (G, tsight-mahs). Tempo.
Zelo (It, dzay-loh). Zeal, ardor.
Zheng. Chinese plucked zither with movable bridges and lacking frets.
Ziemlich (G, tseem'likh). Somewhat, rather.
Zigeunermusik (G, tsee-goy'ner-moo-seek'). Gypsy music.
Zimbalon. Cimbalon.
Zimbel (G, tsim'bell). Cymbal.
Zither. Plucked stringed instrument flat in shape with five melody strings and 27 to 40 open strings that are used for accompaniment.
Zu (G, tsoo). Too, to.
Zug (G, tsook). Slide.
Zunehmend (G, tsoo'nay-mehnt). Increasing, crescendo.
Zunge (G, tsoong-eh). Reed.
Zurückhalten (G, tsoo-rewk'hahl-tn). Direction to hold back, ritard.
Zwei (G, tsvy). Two.
Zwischensatz (G, tsveesh'en-zahts'). Intermediate theme; development section of sonata form.
Zwölftonsystem (G, zvehlf-tohn-zees-tehm). Twelve-tone system (technique).

Composers

This is a comprehensive list of well known composers, but is not necessarily a complete list.

Some composers lived and worked in countries other than where they were born. In significant cases, the first country given is the birthplace, the second country where they lived later.

Adams, John (1947–) U.S.A.
Adler, Samuel (1928–) U.S.A.
Alain, Jehan (1911–1940) France
Albéniz, Isaac (1860–1909) Spain
Alberti, Domenico (1710–1740) Italy
Albinoni, Tomaso (1671–1750) Italy
Alfven, Hugo (1872–1960) Sweden
Antheil, George (1900–1959) U.S.A.
Arensky, Anton (1861–1906) Russia
Arne, Thomas (1710–1778) England
Arnold, Malcolm (1921–) England
Arnold, Samuel (1740–1802) England
Auber, Daniel (1782–1871) France
Babbitt, Milton (1916–) U.S.A.
Bach, Carl Philipp Emanuel (1714–1788) Germany
Bach, Johann Christian (1735–1782) Germany
Bach, Johann Christoph (1642–1705) Germany
Bach, Johann Sebastian (1685–1750) Germany
Bach, Wilhelm Friedemann (1710–1784) Germany
Balakirev, Mily (1837–1910) Russia
Balfe, Michael (1808–1870) Ireland
Bantock, Granville (1868–1946) England
Barber, Samuel (1910–1981) U.S.A.
Bartók, Béla (1881–1945) Hungary
Bax, Arnold (1883–1953) England
Beach, Amy (Mrs. H. H. A.) (1867–1944) U.S.A.
Becker, John (1886–1961) U.S.A.

Beethoven, Ludwig van (1770–1827) Germany
Bellini, Vincenzo (1801–1835) Italy
Benjamin, Arthur (1893–1960) Australia
Bennett, Robert Russell (1894–   ) U.S.A.
Berg, Alban (1885–1935) Austria
Berger, Jean (1905–   ) France–U.S.A.
Berlioz, Hector (1803–1869) France
Bernstein, Leonard (1918–1990) U.S.A.
Billings, William (1746–1800) U.S.A.
Bishop, Henry (1787–1855) England
Bizet, Georges (1838–1875) France
Blacher, Boris (1903–   ) Germany
Blitzstein, Marc (1905–1964) U.S.A.
Bloch, Ernest (1880–1959) Switzerland
Blomdahl, Karl–Birger (1916–1968) Sweden
Blow, John (1649–1708) England
Boccherini, Luigi (1743–1805) Italy
Boely, Alexandre (1785–1858) France
Boito, Arrigo (1842–1918) Italy
Bond, Carrie Jacobs (1862–1946) U.S.A.
Borodin, Alexander (1833–1887) Russia
Boulanger, Lili (1893–1918) France
Boulanger, Nadia (1887–1979) France
Boulez, Pierre (1925–   ) France
Brahms, Johannes (1833–1897) Austria
Britten, Benjamin (1913–1976) England
Bruch, Max (1838–1920) Germany
Bruckner, Anton (1824–1896) Austria
Bull, John (1563–1628) England
Busoni, Ferrucio (1866–1924) Italy
Buxtehude, Dietrich (1637–1707) Germany
Byrd, William (1543–1623) England
Cadman, Charles Wakefield (1881–1946) U.S.A.
Cage, John (1912–1992) U.S.A.
Carissimi, Giacomo (1605–1674) Italy
Carpenter, John Alden (1876–1951) U.S.A.
Carrillo, Julián (1875–1965) Mexico
Carter, Elliott (1908–   ) U.S.A.
Casals, Pablo (1876–1973) Spain—Puerto Rico
Casella, Alfredo (1883–1947) Italy

Castelnuovo-Tedesco–Dufay

Castelnuovo–Tedesco, Mario (1895–1968) Italy
Castro, Juan José (1895–1968) Argentina
Cavalieri, Emilio del (1550–1602) Italy
Chabrier, Emmanuel (1841–1894) France
Chaminade, Cécile (1857–1944) France
Charpentier, Gustave (1860–1956) France
Charpentier, Marc–Antoine (1636–1704) France
Chasins, Abram (1903–1987) U.S.A.
Chausson, Ernest (1855–1899) France
Chavez, Carlos (1899–1978) Mexico
Cherubini, Luigi (1760–1842) Italy
Chopin, Frédéric (1810–1849) Poland
Cilea, Francesco (1866–1950) Italy
Cimarosa, Domenico (1749–1801) Italy
Clarke, Jeremiah (1659–1707) England
Clementi, Muzio (1752–1832) Italy—England
Coleridge–Taylor, Samuel (1875–1912) England
Copland, Aaron (1900–) U.S.A.
Corelli, Arcangelo (1653–1713) Italy
Corigliano, John (1938–) U.S.A.
Couperin, Francois (1668–1733) France
Cowell, Henry (1897–1965) U.S.A.
Creston, Paul (1906–) U.S.A.
Croft, William (1678–1727) England
Crumb, George (1929–) U.S.A.
Czerny, Carl (1791–1857) Austria
Dallapiccola, Luigi (1904–1975) Italy
Debussy, Claude (1862–1918) France
Delibes, Léo (1836–1891) France
Delius, Frederick (1862–1934) England
Dello Joio, Norman (1913–) U.S.A.
Dett, Robert Nathaniel (1882–1943) U.S.A.
Diabelli, Anton (1781–1858) Austria
Diamond, David (1915–) U.S.A.
Dohnányi, Ernst von (1877–1960) Hungary
Donizetti, Gaetano (1797–1848) Italy
Dowland, John (1563–1626) England
Drigo, Riccardo (1846–1930) Italy
Dubois, Theodore (1837–1924) France
Dufay, Guillaume (1400–1474) The Netherlands

Dukas-Glinka

Dukas, Paul (1865–1935) France
Dukelsky, Vladimar (1903–1969) Russia—U.S.A.
DuPré, Marcel (1886–1970) France
Dvořák, Antonín (1841–1904) Bohemia
Elgar, Edward (1857–1934) England
Enesco, Georges (1881–1955) Rumania
Escher, Rudolf (1912–   ) The Netherlands
Falla, Manuel de (1876–1946) Spain
Faure, Gabriel (1845–1924) France
Feldman, Morton (1926–1987) U.S.A.
Ferguson, Howard (1908–   ) Ireland–England
Fernandez, Oscar (1897–1948) Brazil
Fibich, Zdenek (1850–1900) Czechoslovakia
Field, John (1782–1837) Ireland
Fine, Irving (1914–1962) U.S.A.
Finney, Ross Lee (1906–1997) U.S.A.
Finzi, Gerald (1901–1956) England
Flotow, Friedrich von (1812–1883) Germany
Floyd, Carlisle (1926–   ) U.S.A.
Foote, Arthur (1853–1937) U.S.A.
Fortner, Wolfgang (1907–1987) Germany
Foss, Lukas (1922–   ) U.S.A.
Foster, Stephen (1826–1864) U.S.A.
Francaix, Jean (1912–1997) France
Franck, Cesar (1822–1890) Belgium—France
Franz, Robert (1815–1892) Germany
Frescobaldi, Girolamo (1583–1643) Italy
Friml, Rudolf (1879–1972) Czechoslovakia—U.S.A.
Froberger, Johann Jacob (1616–1667) Germany
Gabrieli, Giovanni (1557–1612) Austria
Gabrielli, Domenico (1651–1690) Italy
Ganz, Rudolph (1877–1972) Switzerland—U.S.A.
Gershwin, George (1898–1937) U.S.A.
Giannini, Vittorio (1903–1966) U.S.A.
Gibbons, Orlando (1583–1625) England
Ginastera, Alberto (1916–   ) Argentina
Giordano, Umberto (1867–1948) Italy
Glass, Philip (1937–   ) U.S.A.
Glazunov, Alexander (1865–1936) Russia
Glinka, Mikhail Ivanovich (1804–1857) Russia

141

Gluck-Janáček

Gluck, Christoph (1714–1787) Germany
Godard, Benjamin (1849–1895) France
Goldmark, Karl (1830–1915) Hungary
Goossens, Eugene (1893–1962) England
Gottschalk, Louis (1829–1869) U.S.A.
Gould, Morton (1913–   ) U.S.A.
Gounod, Charles (1818–1893) France
Grainger, Percy (1882–1961) Australia—U.S.A.
Granados, Enrique (1867–1916) Spain
Gretchaninov, Alexander (1864–1956) Russia—U.S.A.
Grieg, Edvard (1843–1907) Norway
Griffes, Charles (1884–1920) U.S.A.
Grofe, Ferde (1892–1972) U.S.A.
Gruenberg, Louis (1884–1964) Russia—U.S.A.
Guarnieri, Camargo (1907–1993) Brazil
Gubaidulina, Sofia (1931–   ) Russia
Gurlitt, Cornelius (1820–1901) Germany
Handel, George (1685–1759) Germany—England
Hanson, Howard (1896–   ) U.S.A.
Harbison, John (1938–) U.S.A.
Harris, Roy (1898–   ) U.S.A.
Harrison, Lou (1917–   ) U.S.A.
Hassler, Hans (1564–1612) Germany
Haydn, Franz Joseph (1732–1809) Austria
Haydn, Michael (1737–1806) Germany
Heller, Stephen (1814–1888) Hungary
Henze, Hans Werner (1926–   ) Germany
Herbert, Victor (1859–1924) Ireland—U.S.A.
Hindemith, Paul (1895–1963) Germany
Holst, Gustav (1874–1934) England
Honegger, Arthur (1892–1955) France
Hovhaness, Alan (1911–   ) U.S.A.
Hummel, Johann Nepomuk (1778–1837) Austria
Humperdinck, Engelbert (1854–1921) Germany
Ibert, Jacques (1890–1962) France
Indy, Vincent d' (1851–1931) France
Ireland, John (1879–1962) England
Ives, Charles (1874–1954) U.S.A.
Jacquet de la Guerre, Elisabeth (1667–1789) France
Janáček, Leoš (1854–1928) Czechoslovakia

Jongen, Joseph (1873–1953) Belgium
Joplin, Scott (1868–1917) U.S.A.
Josquin des Prez (1445–1521) France
Kabalevsky, Dmitri (1904–1987) Russia
Kern, Jerome (1885–1945) U.S.A.
Khatchaturian, Aram (1903–1978) Russia
Kirchner, Leon (1919–   ) U.S.A.
Kodaly, Zoltan (1882–1967) Hungary
Kohler, Louis (1820–1886) Germany
Korngold, Erich Wolfgang (1897–1957) Austria—U.S.A.
Koven, Reginald De (1859–1920) England
Kreisler, Fritz (1875–1962) Austria
Krenek, Ernst (1900–1991) Austria—U.S.A.
Kubik, Gail (1914–1984) U.S.A.
Kuhlau, Friedrich (1786–1832) Germany
Kuhnau, Johann (1660–1722) Germany
Lalo, Edouard (1823–1892) France
Langlais, Jean (1907–   ) France
Lasso, Orlando de (1532–1594) The Netherlands
Lecuona, Ernesto (1895–1963) Cuba
Lehar, Franz (1870–1948) Hungary
Leoncavallo, Ruggiero (1858–1919) Italy
Ligeti, György (1923–   ) Hungary
Liszt, Franz (1811–1886) Hungary
Lloyd Webber, Andrew (1948–   ) England
Loesser, Frank (1910–1969) U.S.A.
Lully, Jean Baptiste (1632–1687) France
Lutoslawski, Witold (1913–   ) Poland
Lutyens, Elisabeth (1906–1983) England
MacDowell, Edward (1861–1908) U.S.A.
Machaut, Guillaume de (1300–1377) France
Maconchy, Elizabeth (1907–1994) England
Mahler, Gustav (1860–1911) Bohemia
Malipiero, Gian Francesco (1882–1973) Italy
Marenzio, Luca (1553–1599) Italy
Martin, Frank (1890–1974) Switzerland
Martinu, Bohuslav (1890–1959) Czechoslovakia
Mascagni, Pietro (1863–1945) Italy
Massenet, Jules (1842–1912) France
Maxwell Davies, Peter (1934–   ) England

Mayuzumi-Ponchielli

Mayuzumi, Toshiro (1929–) Japan
McDonald, Harl (1899–) U.S.A.
Medtner, Nikolai (1879–1951) Russia
Mendelssohn, Felix (1809–1847) Germany
Mennin, Peter (1923–) U.S.A.
Menotti, Gian Carlo (1911–) Italy
Messiaen, Olivier (1908–) France
Meyerbeer, Giacomo (1791–1864) Germany
Miaskovsky, Nikolay (1881–1950) Russia
Milhaud, Darius (1892–1974) France
Monteverdi, Claudio (1567–1643) Italy
Moore, Douglas (1893–1969) U.S.A.
Morley, Thomas (1557–1603) England
Moszkowski, Moritz (1854–1925) Poland—Germany
Mozart, Wolfgang Amadeus (1756–1791) Austria
Mussorgsky, Modest (1839–1881) Russia
Newman, Alfred (1901–1970) U.S.A.
Nielsen, Carl (1865–1931) Denmark
Nicolai, Otto (1810–1849) Germany
Ockeghem, Jean de (1430–1495) Belgium
Offenbach, Jacques (1819–1880) France
Orff, Carl (1895–1982) Germany
Pachelbel, Johann (1653–1706) Germany
Paderewski, Ignace (1866–1941) Poland
Paganini, Niccolo (1782–1840) Italy
Palestrina, Giovanni (1525–1594) Italy
Palmgren, Selim (1878–1951) Finland
Pärt, Arvo (1935–) Estonia
Peeters, Flor (1903–1986) Belgium
Penderecki, Krzyzstof (1933–) Poland
Pergolesi, Giovanni Battista (1710–1736) Italy
Perle, George (1915–) U.S.A.
Persichetti, Vincent (1915–) U.S.A.
Pfitzner, Hans (1869–1949) Germany
Piccinni, Nicola (1728–1800) Italy
Pinto, Octavio (1890–1950) Brazil
Piston, Walter (1894–1976) U.S.A.
Pizzetti, Ildebrando (1880–1968) Italy
Ponce, Manuel (1882–1948) Mexico
Ponchielli, Amilcare (1834–1886) Italy

Porter, Cole (1893–1964) U.S.A.
Poulenc, Francis (1899–1963) France
Prokofiev, Serge (1891–1953) Russia
Puccini, Giacomo (1858–1934) Italy
Purcell, Henry (1659–1695) England
Quantz, Johann (1697–1773) Germany
Rachmaninoff, Serge (1873–1943) Russia
Rameau, Jean Philippe (1683–1764) France
Ravel, Maurice (1875–1937) France
Rawsthorne, Alan (1905–1971) England
Read, Gardner (1913–   ) U.S.A.
Rebikov, Vladimir (1866–1920) Russia
Reger, Max (1873–1916) Germany
Reich, Steve (1936–   ) U.S.A.
Reicha, Antonín (1770–1836) Bohemia
Reinecke, Carl (1824–1910) Germany
Reizenstein, Franz (1911–1968) Germany
Respighi, Ottorino (1879–1936) Italy
Riegger, Wallingford (1885–1961) U.S.A.
Rimsky–Korsakov, Nikolai (1844–1908) Russia
Rodgers, Richard (1902–   ) U.S.A.
Rodrigo, Joaquin (1901–   ) Spain
Romberg, Sigmund (1887–1951) Hungary—U.S.A.
Rorem, Ned (1923–   ) U.S.A.
Rossini, Gioacchino (1792–1868) Italy
Rousseau, Jean–Jacques (1712–1778) Switzerland
Roussel, Albert (1869–1937) France
Rowley, Alec (1892–1958) England
Rubinstein, Anton (1829–1894) Russia
Saint–Saëns, Camille (1835–1921) France
Satie, Erik (1866–1925) France
Scarlatti, Alessandro (1660–1725) Italy
Scarlatti, Domenico (1685–1757) Italy
Schlick, Arnolt (1460–1517) Germany
Schnittke, Alfred (1934–   ) Russia
Schoenberg, Arnold (1874–1951) Austria—U.S.A.
Schubert, Franz (1797–1828) Austria
Schuller, Gunther (1925–   ) U.S.A.
Schuman, William (1910–   ) U.S.A.
Schumann, Robert (1810–1856) Germany

145

Schutz-Varése

Schütz, Heinrich (1585–1672) Germany
Scriabin, Alexander (1872–1915) Russia
Searle, Humphrey (1915–1982) England
Sessions, Roger (1896–1985) U.S.A.
Shostakovich, Dmitri (1906–1975) Russia
Sibelius, Jean (1865–1957) Finland
Siegmeister, Elie (1909–1991) U.S.A.
Sinding, Christian (1856–1941) Norway
Smetana, Bedřich (1824–1884) Bohemia
Soler, Antonio (1729–1783) Spain
Sowerby, Leo (1895–1968) U.S.A.
Speaks, Oley (1874–1948) U.S.A.
Spohr, Ludwig (1784–1859) Germany
Stainer, John (1840–1891) England
Stamitz, Carl (1745–1801) Germany
Stanford, Charles (1852–1924) Ireland
Starer, Robert (1924–   ) U.S.A.
Stevens, Halsey (1908–1989) U.S.A.
Stockhausen, Karlheinz (1928–   ) Germany
Strauss, Johann, Jr. (1825–1899) Austria
Strauss, Richard (1864–1949) Germany
Stravinsky, Igor (1882–1971) Russia—U.S.A.
Sullivan, Arthur (1842–1900) England
Suppé, Franz von (1819–1895) Austria
Sweelinck, Jan (1562–1621) The Netherlands
Szymanowski, Karol (1883–1937) Poland
Takemitsu, Toru (1930–1996) Japan
Tallis, Thomas (1505–1585) England
Tansman, Alexander (1897–   ) Poland
Taylor, Deems (1885–1966) U.S.A.
Tchaikovsky, Peter (1840–1893) Russia
Tcherepnin, Alexander (1899–1978) Russia—U.S.A.
Telemann, Georg (1681–1767) Germany
Thompson, Randall (1899–1984) U.S.A.
Thomson, Virgil (1896–1989) U.S.A.
Tippett, Michael (1905–   ) England
Toch, Ernst (1887–1964) Austria—U.S.A.
Turina, Joaquin (1882–1949) Spain
Turk, Daniel Gottlob (1756–1813) Germany
Varèse, Edgard (1885–1965) France—U.S.A.

Vaughn Williams, Ralph (1872–1958) England
Verdi, Giuseppe (1813–1901) Italy
Villa–Lobos, Heitor (1887–1959) Brazil
Vivaldi, Antonio (1678–1741) Italy
Wagenseil, Georg (1715–1777) Austria
Wagner, Richard (1813–1883) Germany
Waldteufel, Emil (1837–1915) France
Walton, William (1902–   ) England
Weber, Carl Maria von (1786–1826) Germany
Webern, Anton von (1883–1945) Austria
Weill, Kurt (1900–1950) Germany
Widor, Charles (1844–1937) France
Wieniawski, Henri (1835–1880) Poland
Wilbye, John (1574–1638) England
Willan, Healey (1880–1968) Canada
Wolf, Hugo (1860–1903) Austria
Xenakis, Iannis (1922–   ) Greece
Yun, Isang (1917–   ) Korea—Germany
Zemlinsky, Alexander von (1871–1942) Austria
Zwilich, Ellen Taaffe (1939–   ) U.S.A.

Copyright

The 1976 copyright act of the United States provides for copyright in musical compositions. This term includes original compositions consisting of music alone or of words and music combined. It also includes arrangements and other new versions of earlier compositions if new copyrightable work of authorship is added.

Musical works are protected automatically from the moment of creation, meaning the time that they are "fixed" in a tangible form. A work is "fixed" in a tangible medium of expression when its embodiment in a copy or phonorecord is sufficiently permanent or stable to permit it to be perceived, reproduced, or otherwise communicated for a period of more than transitory duration.

Duration of copyright for works created after 1 January 1978 is the composer's life plus seventy years.

The owner of copyrighted musical compositions has certain exclusive rights in his work:

1. to reproduce the copyrighted work in copies or phonorecords;

2. to prepare derivative works based upon the copyrighted work;

3. to distribute copies or phonorecords of the copyrighted work to the public by sale or other transfer of ownership, or by rental, lease, or lending;

4. in the case of literary, musical, dramatic, and choreographic works, pantomimes, and motion pictures and other audiovisual works, to perform the copyrighted work publicly; and

5. in the case of literary, musical, dramatic, and choreographic works, pantomimes, and pictorial, graphic or sculptural works, including the individual images of a motion picture or other audiovisual work, to display the copyrighted work publicly.

Copyright Registration

At any time during the subsistence of copyright, the copyright owner may obtain registration of copyright claim by delivering to the Copyright Office the deposit required ($20.00) together with application form PA. Materials shall include:

1. in the case of an unpublished work, one complete copy or phonorecord;

2. in the case of a published work, two complete copies or phonorecords of the best edition;

3. in the case of a work first published outside the U.S.A., one complete copy or phonorecord as so published;

4. in the case of a contribution of a collective work, one complete copy or phonorecord of the best edition of the collective work.

Notice of Copyright

Whenever a work protected under the law is published in the U.S.A. or elsewhere by authority of the copyright owner, a notice of copyright as provided by this section may be placed on all publicly distributed copies from which the work can be visually perceived, either directly or with the aid of a machine or device. Providing notice of copyright will preclude a subsequent infringer from claiming "innocence" in mitigation of a damage award.

The notice shall consist of three elements:

1. the symbol © (the letter C in a circle) or the word "Copyright" or the abbreviation "Copr.;" and

2. the year of the first publication of the work;

3. the name of the copyright owner, an abbreviation by which the name can be recognized, or a generally known alternative designation of the owner.

Application Form PA is provided by the Copyright Office and may be obtained free upon request. It should be properly completed and signed.

For additional information,

    U.S. Copyright Office
    Library of Congress
    Washington, D.C. 20559

    or

    http://lcweb.loc.gov/copyright